NOT TO ARGUE AND WIN BUT TO KNOW AND TO BE KNOWN

A BLUE SKY STRATEGY

VISWANATHAN C.N.

INDIA · SINGAPORE · MALAYSIA

Notion Press

Old No. 38, New No. 6
McNichols Road, Chetpet
Chennai - 600 031

First Published by Notion Press 2020
Copyright © Viswanathan C.N. 2020
All Rights Reserved.

ISBN 978-1-64850-739-7

"vAgarthAviva sampruktau vAgarthapratipattaye
jagatah pitarau vande pArvatiparameshvarau"-

BRAHMARSHI SREE NARYANA GURU

Dedication

Dedicated to my Father who
dedicated himself to Guru.

Contents

Part Two

THE MANAGEMENT INTERPRETATIONS
OF DARŚANA MĀLĀ

Part Three

EPILOGUE

Acknowledgements

Prayers to God and Brahmarshi Sree Narayana Guru.

Thanks to my immediate family who stood fast by me to do it.

There are two wise men that made this dream become a literary product with the spectacular 'Prologue' and a spontaneous and tranquil 'Introduction' which you are holding now. I would like to thank Teeka Ram Meena, IAS, and Prof. MK Sanoo, unitedly and severally.

Thank you, dear readers for picking up "...*A Blue Sky Strategy.*"

I am indebted to my amazing companions and doubt-clearers – Prof. (Dr.) Santhosh C.R, Sree Narayana College-Chelannur-Kozhikode, and Sajan Menon V, Vazhathodath-East Nada-Triprayar, Kerala, India.

My dear extended families on Social Media, may you accept my gratitude.

The Editor and the entire team at Notion press for being so professional and co-operative through the process.

Purposely put last, but most in the list of importance, Guru Nitya Chaitanya Yati, and his beloved guru, Nataraja Guru, for the seed sown for the present work through their Magnum Opuses – *"The Psychology of Darśana Mālā,* and *"An Integrated Science of the Absolute,"* respectively.

28 February 2020.   – **Viswanathan C.N.**

Foreword

SREE NARAYANA GURU (28 August 1855–20 September 1928), the *Jagat* **Guru**, had written 61 literary marvels which are highly mystic in nature and paramount-philosophical in character. Of them the Gem is *Darśana Mālā,* the '**Celestial Song.**' The inconceivably vast word-creation is a masterpiece of cosmic proportions.

Darśana Mālā, bequeathed to humanity by the great saint, is reading the '**Unitive Vision**' perpetuated by him in his lifetime for the benefit of the Universe. Due to its word-wisdom, it can be approached from any angle according to the view point of the reader. The versatility of the contents of the word-splendour is the very seed of Nataraja Guru's book – *"An Integrated Science of the Absolute."* Nataraja Guru, the favoured disciple of Sree Narayana Guru, used *Darśana Mālā* as a means to reconcile and revalue the philosophical implications of the new Western

Physics. The mystical vision of Guru and the scientific inferences arrived at by the Western physicists and mathematicians of the West come in *pari passu,* in the synthesis-demonstration of the both done by Nataraja Guru, and he concludes that *Darśana Mālā* conceives both the Eastern Spiritualism and the Western Materialism.

The present work, **"NOT TO ARGUE AND WIN BUT TO KNOW AND TO BE KNOWN – A Blue Sky Strategy"** depicts the "Management Aspects" that could be sensed by a perceptive reader of *Darśana* Mālā, on that line of leniency. The author strives his best to draw 'Management Canons' from the words and deeds of Guru Sree Narayana and would like to project the Guru as **"the Leader Immanent"** and the Guru *Sukthas* the precious **'Management Principles.'**

It is not a work of an in-depth study and structural analysis of *Darśana Mālā.* The enthusiasts, students of management and philosophy, and the seekers of Self-awareness and Yoga, and those who are interested in discovering the real *Darśana Mālā* shall first read *"An Integrated Science of the Absolute"* by Nataraja Guru, and *"The Psychology of Darśana Mālā"* of Guru Nitya Chaitanya Yati.

A vertical-horizontal distillation of the epical *Darśana Mālā* done by the author could enable him to incorporate the gross-subtle extracts which are dressed up as 'Strategic Managerial Science' in the work. The author has put in his best effort to ooze out the real contents of the original references so as to add tasty recipe to the work, so that, it could be coined in a rhythmic readable version. The 'uncompromising-absolutist-vision' of Sree Narayana Guru is metamorphosed into "Management Visions" and The Guru's 'Garland Metaphor' is analogized into the 'Aeronautical Metaphor' of "The Stages of Economic Growth" [*The Stages of Economic Growth: A Non-Communist*

Manifesto, **(1960)**]," propounded by Walt Whitman Rostow, the American Economist and the United States' seventh National Security Advisor, in the current work. And the reader may agree that **His All-Holiness Sree Narayana Guru** was a leader Immanent and his preachings and teachings were, are, and will be the high end Management Principles too. In fine, the current work contains *"A Blue Sky Growth Strategy"* to be followed – from birth to final emancipation – by an Individual, a Family, an Organisation, or a Nation.

Welcome to *"Blue Sky Strategy."*

TEEKA RAM MEENA, IAS.

Additional Chief Secretary &
Chief Electoral Officer
Thiruvananthapuram-Kerala.
22 February 2020.

Introduction

Sree Narayana Gurudevan (28 August 1855–20 September 1928), one of the most brilliant mystic philosophers and seers of modern India, is a *Rishi* for some; a Social Reformer for another group; a Spiritual Leader and a Yogi for yet another faction; and a Godly *Avatar* for some other division. These multitudes of belief spark the multi-faceted altitudes of the great Guru and his unique seat in the fabulous *Guruparampara* of Bharat.

"Darśana Mālā," means 'A Garland of Visions,' is the *Magnum Opus* of Sree Narayana Guru. It radiates the incomprehensive and perennial philosophy of high order which is mystical to the core. *"The garland likens consciousness to a series of ten flowers strung together on a golden thread, with a precious jewel pendant in the centre. Each flower is a unitive version, and is described with the utmost economy in ten succinct and evocative verses pregnant with implications"* (indebted to Guru Nitya Chaitanya Yati).

In *Darśana Mālā,* we can see a fusion of the best modern scientific understanding with the traditional wisdom of India's ancient seers. It integrates science and mysticism; it connects Materialism and Spiritualism. It may be the most suited literature to be used by the modern scientific thinkers. The contemplative insight compressed into the lines of *Darśana Mālā* is extracting more symbolic meanings which tend our intellect and intuition and yields an impressive harvest of insight to the reader. It is a must have read master piece of celestial meanings as *Bhagavad Gita.*

Sree Narayana Gurudevan had a very different perspective in pronouncing *Darśana Mālā.* It is the nectar of the persistent contemplation intensely done for years by a *Rishi* in his **'Unitive Vision.'** And it was submitted for the benefit of the whole of the universe. This type of word creation, where wisdom emerges from a holistic appreciation that transcends linear thinking and logical interpretation, is called *Darsana.* It is a philosophically presented mystical vision.

Guru's teachings contain a summation of science and spirituality. Science uncovers the deepest truths, while spirituality is the search for the cause behind fact. Scientists search through outer gadgets, whereas the spiritualists focus on higher levels of consciousness. Both the science and spirituality aim at the same truth, but they arrive at there differently. Physical scientists gaze at the stars through telescopes at the observatories and listen to radio waves from distant stars, while spiritual scientists aim at the inner horizon listening to the inner music of the spheres through yogic meditation. Briefly, the both go parallel to each other. Challenging this notion, Nataraja Guru demonstrates the synthesis between the highly mystical vision of his Guru (Sree Narayana Guru) and the scientific findings of the West and he reconciles and re-values the philosophical implications of Western physics by means of *Darśana Mālā.*

The present work, **"NOT TO ARGUE AND WIN BUT TO KNOW AND TO BE KNOWN – A Blue Sky Strategy,"** is an analogy between 'Sree Narayana Guru-Philosophy' and 'Management Principles.' The author has gone through an unbeaten path to make fission to ferret out the intrinsic secrets concealed in the indecipherable and mystic *vedantic* thoughts of a sage so as to define new generation Management Canons.

The ten *Darśanas* in Guru's *Darśana Mālā* have been equated to Ten Management Visions, and each *Darsana is* explained in Modern Management Terms. The work is presented as a Management Commentary upon *Darśana Mālā,* rather than a complicated analytic or synthetic cross pollination. It is a maiden attempt of its nature. The reader may feel it as a fiction or perhaps stranger than fiction. The reader may not attempt to seek the verticality of its truth or go for any acid tests for its practicality; instead may try to know and to be known.

Guru's literary works are commonly a fusion of the best of modern scientific understanding with the traditional *Rishic*-ascetic wisdom of India. Hence, they can be explained, equated, evaluated or re-evaluated in manifold ways subject to the individual fancies of the reader. "Guru Philosophy" is the summation of scientific skepticism and spiritual accepticism. It contains hectic materialism and pacific religious theism. Orienting such a philosophy to Management Principles is a well-nigh Herculean task. The journey from the 'Absolutist Perspective' to the 'New Generation Management Science' is rather a cumbersome exercise of walking down across the rocky-slippery-slope above the Grand Canyon.

Transmuting the indistinguishable philosophical knots of structuralism revived by Sree Narayana Guru, in order to give birth to a Management Philosophy, is a daunting mission. Nonetheless, the author has shown his dexterity and firm conviction to face the odyssey.

The author has extracted symbolic meanings from Guru's 'Metaphor of a Garland,' with a view to sprout a branch to embrace the 'Aeronautical Metaphor' of Walt Whitman Rostow, the American Economist.

Briefly, the work is in three parts. **Part one is 'The Text in Translation' of *Darśana Mālā* (copied from '*The Psychology of Darśanamala*', Nitya Chaitanya Yati, Gurukula Publishing House, Fernhill – Varkala – Bainbridge, 1987). This is not a part of the structure of the work, and it is given with the good intention of familiarising *Darśana Mālā* (English Translation) to the readers.**

The Part Two and Part Three are the real text of the present work. The Part Two deals with the 'Introspection and the Remergence' of the Ten *Darśanas* of *Darśana Mālā*. It is done in Ten Chapters: each chapter is given for each *Darsana*. The Part Three is THE GURU EFFECT which consists of two sections: the first fragment reads the diagnostic versions of the wisdom of Guru in Management terms and their influences that have been felt by the author; the second segment contains the glimpses of renowned personalities about the Guru.

Rationalist thinker may differ; empiricist reader may negotiate; a perceptive student may sign up; commons may nod off. Nevertheless, let me introduce this work to you all for your invaluable evaluations.

M.K.Sanoo

PROF. M.K. SANOO
Sandhya, Ernakulam.   **22 February 2020.**

Author's Note

BRAHMARSHI SREE NARAYANA GURU (28 August 1855 – 20 September 1928) is metamorphosed as **"THE MANAGER"** (better say, **"THE IMMANENT LEADER"**) and the Guru's literary creations, preachings, teachings, and his very being are narrated picturesque as **"MANAGEMENT PRINCIPLES,"** in this book.

The Guru went perpendicular through Indian philosophy, making a *Bhashya (Bhashyam)* – a 'Commentary or Exposition' – to the *'Advaitha Sidhanta'* of *Adi Sankara*, and established laymen's philosophy which has rooted deep in the Indian psyche. This is *'Advaitha 2.0.'* The Guru's *Advaitha philosophy* is a piece of *'Indian Management Thought.'*

"Do unto others as you would have them do unto you" – the core of the "Sermon on the Mount" by **Jesus** – has been expressed by the Guru in simple words as: *"Avanavan – athma – sughathin – aa – charikkunnava Apārannu – sughathinayi – varenam"*. *'All things, whatsoever, ye would that men should do to you, do ye even so to them'* – The 'Mosaic Law' – is read the other way as: *"Whatever is harmful to you, do not do to any other person"*. This Golden Rule is the bed-rock of the 'Central Ethical Teachings' of **Sree Narayana Guru.**

The present work is the equation of Guru's *Darśana Mālā* into modern 'Management Philosophy.' It explains the Gurujian Morality, values and Inventions. These values have taken roots deep in the society, creating an overall change in the general Indian psyche. It has been set in the heart, mind, and consciousness of India. A plethora of social movements arose from attempts to improve the prevailing harsh living conditions for many under a rigid class system. The Gurujian Morality has been instrumental for the changes. Roughly speaking, the Georgian Morality (1714–1837), the Victorian Morality (1837–1901), and the Gurujian Morality (1856–1928) were the code of conducts of people in their respective periods in India. Bharat, one of the most ancient of civilisations in the world is poised at a very crucial phase with multiple challenges now. And the Grand Panacea is the Gurujian Morality.

There are 60+1 literary creations of Guru in Malayalam, Sanskrit and Tamil languages of which *Darśana Mālā* assumes a prominent status. Once, Prof. (Dr) Sukumar Azhikode had aptly qualified **Darśana Mālā** as *"Bhagavad Gita in Malayalam."* Absolutely it is true. The mystic in-depth and the fathomless multitude of Rishic ascetics' pregnancy in letter forms in *Darśana Mālā* deserve the pendant-qualification – *"Bhagavad Gita-the-Second (Bhagavad Gita 2.0).* Darśana Mālā* is the *magnum opus* of Sree Narayana Guru. It radiates the Gurjian Morality, values, and "philosophical-inventions-the-rare," which have taken roots deep in the society, creating an overall change in the general Indian psyche. The Gurujian Morality has been set in the heart, mind and consciousness of India.

The present work is the equation of Guru's *Darśana Mālā* into modern Managerial Science. It explains the Gurujian Mortality, values and philosophical inventions so as to equate them to 'New Gen Management Principles.

The Darśana Mālā or **"Garland of Visions"** is the 'Manifesto of Indian Philosophy.' It is an amalgam of science and spirituality. Guru's teachings contain a summation of science and spirituality as integral parts. *Darśana Mālā* consists of

100 verses, divided into ten chapters of ten versus each. *"Each chapter is a vision, complete in itself, and also forming part of the greater whole."* [Nitya Chaitanya Yati, (1987), *"The Psychology of Darśanamala"*].

"Towards the end of his life, in 1916, Guru was asked by his disciples for a definitive work on Vedanta philosophy. Then he agreed to do under certain guidelines. He would chant the work (in Sanskrit) and Swami Vidyananda was to take it down. There were to be no repetition. If he was asked for any, he would stop. The disciples agreed to the conditions".

"Early in the day, the Guru would go for a walk, and Swami Vidyananda accompanied carrying his water pot. With the swami's hands thus engaged, Narayana Guru chanted ten verses, which Vidyananda would have to commit to memory. When the Guru finally took his water pot and wandered into the jungle, the swami would immediately sit down and begin writing feverishly. Thus, even the production of this timeless master-piece was used as a tool to further the training of a disciple".

*"After this routine was repeated several times, Narayana Guru said simple: "That's all." He then asked Swami Vidyananda to read the verses back to him and he gave his tacit approval. Finally, Guru told his disciples that there were ten visions, gave their names, and titled the work **"Darśana Mālā."***** [Nitya Chaitanya Yati (1987): *"The Psychology of Darśanamala"*, Gurukula Publishing House, Fernhill – Varkala – Kerala, First impression, pp6,&7, INTRODUCTION, Scott Teitsworth, Portland, Oregon].

Darśana Mālā is **"The Song Celestial."** It is a Sanskrit Epic depicting the conflicts in the human mind, social behaviour, and philosophical being. It is a script to be read, understood, and internalised. It is a treasure of pearls of wisdom, and for the learned it is the **"philosophical ultimate in learning."**

"Darśanam is a general term for perception. The *Darśanams* (perceptions) pronounced by Narayana Guru in Sanskrit stimulate human senses beyond any limit. They are incomprehensive to the average brains. The perceptive vastness of the philosophical work costs its popularity. It is an un-mined treasure of intellectual gem of the purest ray serene that the dark unfathomed caves of philosophical ocean bear.

Given below are the Ten *Darśanas* from Sree Narayana Guru's *Darśana Mālā:*

ADHYĀROPA DARŚANAM	:	*VISION* OF *SUPPOSITION*
APAVĀDA DARŚANAM	:	*VISION OF TRUTH*
ASATYA DARŚANAM	:	*VISION* OF *NON-EXISTENCE*
MĀYĀ DARŚANAM	:	*VISION OF NEGATION*
BHĀNA DARŚANAM	:	*VISION OF AWARENESS*
KARMA DARŚANAM	:	*VISION* OF *ACTION*
JÑĀNA *DARSANAN*	:	*VISION OF CONSCIOUSNESS*
BHAKTI DARŚANAM	:	*VISION* OF *CONTEMPLATION*
YOGA DARŚANAM	:	*VISION OF UNION*
NIRVĀNA DARŚANAM	:	*VISION* OF *EMANCIPATION*

Narayana Guru dictated the work, *Darśana Mālā,* in Sanskrit. Its original publication was in Malayalam language. Nataraja Guru, the disciple of Narayana Guru and the founder of the Narayana Gurukula, translated the entire poem into English in 1948–49. Guru Nitya Chaitanya Yati wrote a book entitled *"The Psychpology of Darśana Mālā"* in 1987, based on the translated work of Nataraja Guru. The Socrates – Plato – Aristotelian trio is manifested in the triumvirate of Sree Narayana Guru – Nataraja Guru – Guru Nitya Chaitanya Yati, in India.

"The *Psychology of Darśana Mālā* of Guru Nitya Chaitanya Yati (1987) is the Original Work on which the present work is based on."

Our habitual mode of thinking fails to grasp the 'word-wisdom' projected in *Darśana Mālā*. The *Darśana Mālā* is a multi-dimensional solid whereas our minds tend to follow a one-dimensional line which fails an intensive effort in an unaccustomed direction in order to penetrate to the core of it. Assimilating *Darśana Mālā* is a concentrated process and that is the reason why the great epic-like work is remaining unappreciated masterpiece. The mystery of the work's content could be digested only by a seeker of wisdom bent on self-improvement. One cannot hope to have it all by a casual perusal and thought. In fine, **Darśana Mālā** is a textbook of the **"Science of the Absolute"**, containing the pith of the blend of science and philosophy.

The different *Darśanas* define different forms of "Management Strategies." They explain and expound different forms of visions. Guru's metaphor of a garland is a seed or kernel which, when nursed and tended by the students' intellect and intuition, yields an impressive harvest of insight. Here, the author is engaged in theorizing the Guru's philosophy so as to equate it to modern 'Management Thoughts.' It is an attempt of metamorphosing of Guru's saintly visions into "Management Visions" which the reader may feel stranger an attempt. The "First Law of Thermodynamics," also known as "Law of Conservation of Energy" states that *"Energy can neither be created nor destroyed; energy can only be transferred or changed from one form to another."* Akin to this law, here the author attempts to 'transform' the Guru's Visions in *Darśana Mālā* to ' Management Visions' by interpreting the views and the ethical values conceived in them, in a clinical precision.

Walt Whitman Rostow (1916 – 2003), American Economist and the United States' seventh National Security Advisor, released a historical Model of Economic Growth (**"The Stages of Economic Growth, A non-Communist Manifesto"**), in 1960. The model postulates that every economy passes through the five basic stages of economic growth in varying length. The stages are: **The Traditional Society; The Pre-conditions for Take-Off; The Take-Off; The Drive to Maturity; and The Age of High Mass Consumption.** Rostow has given it as a simile of flight of an aircraft.

There are 10 phases of flight of an Aircraft in its Flight Cycle: Fuelling and Embarkation; Taxiing to the runway; Performing for Take-Off; Take-Off; Climb; Cruise; Descent; Final Approach; Landing; and Disembarkation. The present work is an analogy between this 'Aeronautical Metaphor' and the Gurujian 'Garland Metaphor,' with a sacred view of ferreting out the intrinsic intricacies of 'Management Concepts' hidden in *Darśana Mālā*. The 10 *Darśanas* given in *Darśana Mālā* are manifested as **"10 Management Visions and Theories"** in the current work. Though Rostow has cut short the flight cycle of an economy into Five Stages (for making it comprehensive), it has given an impetus to the author to theorize the "Gurujian Model of Life Cycle" (the 10 stages in 10 *Darśanas)* into a ten-stage "Management Cycle of an Industrial Organisation."

This work constitutes three Parts. The 'PART ONE' is the 'THE TEXT IN TRANSLATION' of Darśana Mālā. It is a copy from '*The Psychology of Darśana Mālā,*' Nitya Chaitanya Yati, Gurukula Publishing House, Fernhill-Varkala-Bainbridge, (1987). The PART ONE does not constitute the structure of the work; it is given with a genuine thought of familiarising the *Darśana Mālā,* in its English Translation form, to the readers.

The 'PART TWO' – THE MANAGEMENT INTERPRETATIONS OF DARŚANA MĀLĀ – contains 'Ten Chapters' and 'Sum Up.' Each chapter bears a *Darśanam* (in the chronological order of Ten *Darśanams* of *Darśana Mālā)*. The first part of each chapter contains the Guru's narratives about the respective Darsana and its Management Concepts are elucidated in the next part.

The 'PART THREE' reads Epilogue. It is bifurcated into part A and part B. The part A, "THE GURU EFFECT," is the diagnostic versions of the wisdom of Guru in Management Terms and their influences which have been experienced, assumed and felt by the author. Part B contains the glimpses of renowned personalities and Organisations about the Guru which are substantiating and supporting the author's views.

Owing to its seminal nature, *Darśana Mālā* can be approached from many different points of view and angles. Here, it is an attempt to abridge and amplify the "Management Aspects" in Guru's *Magnum Opus* and to synthesise its mystical versions and the scientific wisdoms. It is a commentary and examination; not an intellectual fancy.

May the reader maintain an attitude of healthy scepticism and critical scrutiny?

Hopefully, let me submit this work at the lotus feet of Brahmarshi Sree Narayana Guru.

– Author

Part One

DARŚANA MĀLĀ

(THE TEXT IN TRANSLATION)

I. ADHYĀROPA DARŚANAM

1. It was in the beginning as if non-existence –
   this world, like a dream; thereafter,
   everything was projected
   by the will alone of the Supreme Lord.

2. As incipient memory from alone, in the beginning,
   this remained ; thereafter, the Lord
   projected with his *MĀYĀ*
   like a magician, the entire world.

3. Before origination this was
   latent in him; thereafter, from him,
   as sprout from seed, by his own
   power it created itself alone.

4. The power, however, is of two kinds, known as
   the bright and the dark; thus,
   there is no existence between these,
   as with light and darkness.

5. This, of mind-stuff alone, in the beginning
   was accomplished, as if a painting,
   with all the picturesqueness seen here,
   by the Lord, like an artist.

6. Like potential yogic power,
   in the beginning this was nature indeed;
   thereafter, like a yogi, the Lord of the World
   unfolded his magical powers.

7. When Self-knowledge shrinks,
   then ignorance is fearful;
   substantiation by name and form,
   in the most terrible fashion, looms here, ghost-like.

8. This is terrible and empty of content,
   like a phantom city;
   even as such, the whole universe
   is made as a wonder by the Primeval One.

9. From the sun, by stages, was not at all
   how the world came to be; from the Self
   this appeared all at once,
   as one's vision comes in sleep.

10. He from whom this world manifested,
    as a fig tree from a seed –
    he is Brahma, he is Siva and Vishnu,
    he is the Absolute, he alone is all.

II. APAVĀDA DARŚANAM

1. This world, which is of gross
   and subtle form, comes from consciousness;
   if it is affirmed everything is existence through and through;
   if it is denied, it is consciousness through and through.

2. Apart from cause there is no effect;
   therefore, all this is unreal;
   for the unreal, how can there be an origin?
   Of the originated, what dissolution?

3. That which has no origin or dissolution
   is none other than the supreme Absolute;
   through *MĀYĀ* the confusion arises that there is
   origin and dissolution in the Self.

4. Because of its non-difference from cause,
   how can an effect come to an existence?
   By that how can there be
   the non-existence of cause also?

5. This which is unreal, being an effect,
   has a cause; it is not the world,
   but the Absolute that alone is real,
   which a dull mind wrongly imagines to be unreal.

6. If one alone has reality,
   how can one experience another's beingness?
   To say that the real is in the real is tautology;
   to say it is in the unreal is contradiction.

7. When all parts are separated
   one by one, then one sees
   everything as consciousness alone –
   far from *MĀYĀ* – and not any other.

8. Consciousness alone, not another, shines;
   therefore there is n nothing other than consciousness;
   what does not shine – that is unreal;
   and what is unreal – that does not shine.

9. *Ananada* alone shines as real,
   not anything else; therefore, everything
   is *ananada* through and through;
   apart from *ananda* nothing else is known.

10. All is indeed existence, consciousness, and pure happiness;
    in this there is not even a trace of the many;
    he who sees this as many
    goes from death to death.

III. ASATHYA DARŚANAM

1. All this is a permeation of mind,
   but mind is nowhere to be seen;
   in the same way, like blue and so on in the sky,
   the world is seen in the Self.

2. By ignorance, which is none other than the mind,
   all worlds are imagined;
   when by this knowledge dissolution comes,
   then everything becomes like a painting.

3. What expands here from darkness
   into a ghost to a coward –
   that world is seen by the wise
   as a dream-world of the wakeful state.

4. The visible is imagined by the will;
   the visible is seen only where there is will,
   and not where there is no will–
   like the snake in the rope.

5. There is no difference between will
   and mind; that mind, which is called
   ignorance and darkness, is a wonder,
   like Indra's magic.

6. To one who reasons correctly
   the world appears as a mirage in the Self;
   and to the indiscriminate, by confusion,
   a reflection looks as if it is real.

7. The Self does not, like milk, attain
   to another form; therefore, everything
   as in the creation by Indra's magic,
   seems to be through superimposition.

8. *MĀYĀ* alone is the primal cause of the world;
   by that which is none other than the
   wielder of *MĀYĀ* all this is created,
   like the unreal effects of psychic powers.

9. To the mature mind of the old the world appears
   in the Self as a forest in the sky,
   even as the unreal form of a puppet
   seems otherwise to a child.

10. The One is real, not a second;
    the unreal indeed appears to be real;
    the *sivalingam* is stone alone,
    not a second made by the sculptor.

IV. MĀYĀ DARŚANAM

1. What is not known, that is Māyā;
   it alone shines as many forms:
   vidya, avidya, para, apāra,
   tamas, pradhana, and prakrit.

2. Like the prior non-existence in the day alone, before it is fashioned,
   none other than the Absolute is known;
   what is that Absolute is indeed
   MĀYĀ, of indeterminate possibility.

3. The non-Self is unreal, the Self is real;
   thus, the means by which such knowledge comes,
   that is this *vidya*, like the recognition
   of the truth about rope and snake.

4. The Self is unreal, the non-Self is real;
   Thus, the means by which such knowledge comes,
   that alone is *avidya,* like the erroneous cognition
   about rope as a snake.

5. The senses, mind, intelligence,
   five vital tendencies and such – that by which
   they are specifically created as the subtle limbs
   of the reasoning Self is *para* alone.

6. Adopting these limbs, the reasoning Self
   by its own *MĀYĀ* becomes deluded,
   as if happy and unhappy;
   in truth there is nothing at all.

7. That by which this world, which is indeed
   the object of the senses, is specifically created
   is *apāra* alone, which in the Self
   permeates the eidetic imagery of the gross.

8. As ignorance of mother-of-pearl
   is the basis of silver,
   what is imagined in the Self –
   that is known as *tamas*.

9. Just as a tree is wonderfully
   latent in the seed,
   all are in this; therefore, or by its
   importance, it is called *pradhanam*.

10. As by its very nature it
    diversifies the modalities marvellously,
    this, of three-fold modality,
    is well-known here as *prakrit*.

V. BHĀNA DARŚANAM

1. Present within as without,
   constantly fluttering like a bee,
   awareness is divided into just two kinds:
   generic and specific.

2. Gross, subtle, causal, and the fourth –
   thus, the bases of awareness are of four kinds;
   the same names
   apply to awareness also.

3. See here: "I am the body;
   this is a pot." Thus, based on the gross,
   the awareness which is experienced,
   that is considered to be the gross.

4. Here, such awareness as "body" and "pot",
   these are the specific;
   similarly, "I,""this," and such
   are to be remembered as the generic.

5. The senses, mind, intellect,
   items of interest, and five vital breaths –
   the awareness which constitutes
   the subtle nature of its basis is the subtle.

6. "I am ignorant" – such awareness
   exemplifies the causal;
   here, what is revealed as "I am" is the generic,
   "ignorant" is the specific.

7. "I am the Absolute" – such awareness
   is praised as the fourth;
   here, the element "I am" is the generic,
   and "the Absolute" is the specific.

8. Where there is awareness, there is an object of awareness';
   where there is no awareness, there is no object of awareness;
   thus, by agreement,
   and also by difference, certitude comes.

9. As the eye does not see itself, even so
   the Self by the self; because the Self is not
   an object of awareness, what the Self sees –
   that indeed is the object of awareness.

10. What is the object of awareness, that is superimposed;
    the non-superimposed is not an object of awareness;
    what is superimposed, that is unreal;
    what is not superimposed – That alone is real.

VI. KARMA DARŚANAM

1. The Self, through *Māyā,* does
   action by assuming many forms,
   though detached and self-luminous,
   like the *taijasa* in sleep.

2. I think, I speak, I grasp, I hear –
   all such forms of action are done
   by the Supreme Self
   through the agency of consciousness and the *indriya-s.*

3. Prior to action the Self alone is;
   nothing else is known;
   therefore, actions are done
   by itself with its own *MĀYĀ.*

4. The Self has some kind of power,
   inseparable from it, difficult to define;
   by that alone all actions are
   projected in the action-less Self.

5. The Self is always detached alone;
   by ignorance action is done as if attached;
   "I am not acting" – thus,
   the seer remains detached in action.

6. The one Self alone
   burns as fire, blows as wind,
   showers as rain, supports
   as earth, and flows as river.

7. Going upward as *prana,*
   downward as *apana,*
   remaining actionless, the one alone
   beats, murmurs, and pulsates in the nerves.

8. From the unmodulating Self,
   and not another, the six aspects –
   existence, birth, growth, change,
   deterioration, and extinction – happen here.

9. In spite of action becoming self-accomplished
   by the psychic dynamism and the senses,
   the wise one knows, "I am the
   unattached *kutastha.*"

10. Because "I" is seen as an object of
    awareness, I-consciousness is also a superimposition,
    like the silver in the mother-of-pearl;
    above everything else, today and tomorrow, the one alone exists.

VII. JÑĀNA DARŚANAM

1. Knowledge is one indeed – unconditioned
   and conditioned; that, devoid of
   I-consciousness and so on,
   is the knowledge which is unconditioned.

2. That knowledge modulated as I-consciousness inside,
   likewise that which is modulated
   as knowledge of thisness outside,
   such knowledge is known as the conditioned.

3. That by which one experiences the witnessing of the non-Self,
   such as I-consciousness and so on,
   is Self-knowledge, by which alone
   immortality is enjoyed.

4. That by which I-consciousness and innumerable
   such effects, which being to the non-Self,
   are known, is said to be
   knowledge of the non-Self.

5. When things are known as they are,
   as in the knowledge of the truth of rope,
   that is factual knowledge;
   and fictitious when it is otherwise.

6. By the mere presence of which alone
   everything is illuminated –
   that is characterised as knowledge of
   immediate perception, and also as inner perception.

7. That form of the modulation
   of knowledge, by which the appraisal of
   the possibility produced by concomitant inherence
   is deduced, is inference.

8. On going near the object to be ascertained
   and recognising, "this is the form of the animal
   whose marks have been heard of" – that by which
   such knowledge comes is analogy.

9. The knowledge of "I am," "mine," and so on,
   is individual knowledge;
   the other, such as "that," "this," and so on,
   is spoken of as sensory knowledge.

10. *Aum tat sat* – what is thus instructed,
    arrived at as the union of the Absolute and the Self,
    devoid of functions like willing –
    that is said to be absolute knowledge.

VIII. BHAKTI DARŚANAM

1. Meditation on the Self is b*hakthi.*
   That by which the Self is blissful, with that,
   the knower of the Self always meditates
   upon the Self by the Self.

2. *Brahma* is meditated upon
   because *Brahma* is blissful.
   Constant meditation on *Brahma*
   is known as *bhakti.*

3. *Ananda* alone is meditated,
   not misery by anyone any time.
   That meditation which is blissful
   is bhakti, it is instructed.

4. *Atma a*lone is *Brahma.*
   The knower of the Self contemplates the *atma,* not any other.
   This thus meditating the Self
   is named as *bhakti.*

5. *Ananada, atma,* and *Brahma* –
   such are the names of this alone, so it is said.
   In whom there is such certitude of awareness,
   he as a contemplative is well known.

6. I am *ananda*, I am *Brahma*, I am *atma;*
   in such forms, for whom
   there is always identification,
   as a contemplative he is well known.

7. The wife does not merely worship the husband,
   nor the husband, the wife.
   By all, their *ananda* alone is worshiped,
   which resides in the sense interests.

8. Thus the wise man sees everywhere
   nothing but the joy of the Self –
   not even a little of anything else.
   His *bhakti* indeed is the highest.

9. Towards the Father of the world,
   to one's spiritual teacher, father, mother,
   towards the founders of truth,
   towards those who walk in the same path.

10. towards those who put down evil,
    (and) to those who do good to all,
    what sympathy there is, that is *bhakti,*
    what here belonging to the supreme Self is the ultimate.

IX. YOGA DARŚANAM

1. That which always unites
   and also gets united with *cidatma,*
   which is in the form of restraining mind,
   that is praised as *yoga.*

2. Where the seer, the sight and the seen
   are not known, there the heart
   should be joined while *vāsana* is present.
   Such is *yoga* – thus the *yoga*-knower.

3. All this name and form is
   Brahma indeed. Thus, in
   the Absolute, mind always merges well.
   This is ascertained as *yoga.*

4. By the modulation of consciousness
   which is unbroken as in the streak of oil,
   what incessant rejoicing is in the Self.
   Such is *yoga* – this is the recognition of *yogi-s.*

5. To whichever mind goes, from all that
   this should always be restrained,
   and should be united in the Self –
   this is *yoga.* In this should remain united.

6 & 7. *Sankalpa*– the cause of all disasters of mankind –
   along with projections, should be uprooted
   and incipient memories be restrained in the *atma*.
   What is seen has not the perceived
   reality, because what is seen
   is the seer itself. Who is thus united
   in the seer, he is the best among yoga-knowers.

8. When mind, the bumble bee, sips
   the honey-like sweetness of one's own bliss,
   fluttering ceases and is drawn
   into union by *yoga vayu*.

9. When meditation is done with gaze between the eyebrows
   and the tip of the tongue fixed above the uvula,
   then happens *khecari mudra,*
   which dispels torpor and fatigue.

10. In this world yoga, in short, is of
    two forms – knowledge and *karma* – thus.
    All forms of *yoga* are conclusively comprised
    in these two descriptions of *yoga*.

X. NIRVĀNA DARŚANAM

1. *NIRVĀNA* is of two kinds:
   the pure and the impure.
   That which is the pure is devoid of *vāsana;*
   similarly, that is impure which is conjoined with *vāsana.*

2. Most pure, pure – thus
   the pure is of two kinds, and similarly
   the impure also is said to be
   impure pure and impure-impure.

3. The most pure is again of three kinds:
   one in the superior, one in the more superior,
   one in the most superior; and thus
   the pure is established in the *brahma*-knower.

4. The impure-pure is devoid of *rajas* and *tamas*
   and the other is with *rajas* and *tamas.*
   The former is known to be the seeker of liberation,
   the latter in those who desire psychic attainment.

5. Having burned everything with the fire of wisdom,
   aiming the good of the world,
   doing action according to injunction,
   the knower of *brahma* remains firm in *brahma.*

6. Having renounced all action,
   always established in the Absolute,
   who moves about the world merely to conduct bodily life –
   he is the superior knower of *brahma.*

7. He knows only when informed by another,
   does not know by himself –
   such a person is the more superior.
   He always enjoys absorption in the Absolute.

8. Not knowing anything by himself,
   even when informed he remains so –
   such a person is the most superior.
   Always without modulation, he is *brahma* alone.

9. Of this, there is nothing avoidable and acceptable.
   As for the Self, it shines by itself.
   Thus having become certain, liberate.
   Thereafter modulation does not repeat.

10. The one *brahma* alone is without a second;
    nothing else is; there is no doubt.
    Thus the knower should liberate from duality.
    Thereafter he does not return. **(THE END)**

(N.B: Totally indebted to "*THE PSYCHOLOGY OF DARŚANA MĀLĀ,*" NITYA CHAITANYA YATI, GURUKULA PUBLISHING HOUSE, FERNHILL-VARKALA-BAINBRIDGE, 1987).

Part Two

THE MANAGEMENT
INTERPRETATIONS OF
DARŚANA MĀLĀ

Chapter 1

ADHYĀROPA DARŚANAM

Meaning:

The dichotomy of mankind consists of Spiritualists and Materialists.

The spiritualists believe: *"Brahma, Vishnu, Maheswara* – the Trinity is One. He is the Ultimate; everything is He, indeed. He from whom, like a fig tree as from seed, came out this world manifested. Like a *Yogi,* did He, the Lord of the world, worked out His varied psychic powers, like a magician, created this entire world. The whole Universe was latent within Him. Thereafter, dream-wise, like an artist, everything existent created He, the Lord Supreme." The one Supreme Truth which generates, sustains, and dissolves is described *Brahma, Vishnu*, and *Siva*, respectively.

The Spiritualists argue that, "In the beginning, the world was non-existent like a dream; thereafter, everything was projected by the will alone of the Supreme Lord. In the beginning, the world was remained as an incipient memory forms; thereafter, the Lord projected the entire world with His *Māyā,* like a magician does. In the beginning, it was latent in Him; thereafter, from Him alone it sprouted. In the beginning, it was a mind-stuff alone; thereafter, as an artist, He painted it out with all the picturesqueness that is seen now. In the beginning, it was like a potential yogic power, the nature indeed; thereafter, like a yogi, the Lord of the world unfolded his magical powers to emerge it."

As in the stages of the unfoldment of a tree – seed, germination, first sprout, the growth of branches, emergence of flowers, the final fruition, and the extinction-last – all the developments arise from the tree itself as put everything inherent and is not the effect of any external cause. The root descends into the earth, heliotropically oriented, in search of water, salts, and minerals; the other part performs its functions geotropically. Thus the metabolic function of the tree takes place in two environments of light and darkness, in its existence.

Now, here, it is the take of Materialists: "There is a mythological story in which the Sun gave birth to Space. Space then gave birth to Air, air gave birth to Fire, and fire gave birth to Water, and from water came the Earth." Modern science theorises about the formation of the Universe in a somewhat similar manner when it speaks of an un-identified energy yet, passing through a series of modifications on its way to becoming manifest as this planet. This energy is expressed as '*nebula*' which becomes a star; the explosion of the star forms a planetary system; and finally the cooling of the planetary fires allows water and other liquids to condense, leading to the development of an environment and atmosphere conducive to the manifestation of life on the planet.

However, both the groups are sincerely trying to remove the wrongly indoctrinated convictions and to establish truths. In that course of action, they consciously try to super-impose their views over others. This super-imposition, in Sanskrit, is called *ADHYĀROPA*.

Dormant concepts, incipient memories, and psychological urges give birth to various thoughts which may be true partially and wrong partially. Mere personal conviction is not sufficient to validate truth. It is a super-imposition. Super-imposition means the transposition or imposition of something alien and strange which remains beyond our comprehension. *ADHYĀROPA* means super-imposition.

What is there before anything is experienced? Answer is nothing. Out of 'nothingness' comes 'thingness' to us. So, what is nothing? It is the prior absence of 'things.' Before a pot is made out of clay, there is a prior absence of it in the clay. The prior absence of the pot is the nothingness of it, and from that absence arises the 'thingness' of it. Thus, if something has to come, there has to be a possibility of it, but that prior possibility remains unknown. All our experiences have their prior absences in that unknown which is the ground of all and we must seek and find it out.

A vital urge is required for unlocking the hidden reservoirs of inner forces to ferret out the truth. The negative and the positive, the dark (*tamasi*), and the bright (*taijasi*), *Yin* and *Yang,* interplay and interlace in different degrees in all forms of manifestations.

Management Concepts of *Adhyāropa Darśanam*

[VISION OF SUPPOSITION]

(The Ability to Project an Image of Oneself Across Time and Space)

"It is not in the stars to hold our destiny, but in ourselves."

– William Shakespeare

Adhyāropa Darśanam is called 'Vision of Supposition.' It is also known as 'Vision of Cosmic Projection.'

An 'Entrepreneur' is *Brahma, Vishnu, and Maheshwara* of his enterprise. A business is latent in a business man as a dream. He is literally a *Yogi*. He is an artist. He paints his imagination in all the picturesque rapidity. The idea of business sprouts from his mind, slowly grows, and passes through various stages of its existence, as in the stages of unfoldment of a tree – seed, germination, first sprout, the growth of branches, emergence of flowers, and the final fruition.

"*I am One, let me become many*", (*Chandogya Upanishad*). Similarly, a businessman is one but he manifests himself in many forms – organiser, producer, marketer, employer, leader, manger... The business idea is latent within him, it comes out in different colours. He is the *Brahma, Vishnu,* and *Siva* of his business: like *Brahma,* he makes ideation; like *Vishnu,* he nourishes it; like *Siva,* he closes it down. He is the creator, nourisher, and himself is the annihilator too. The 'Universal Prayer' (*Daiva Dasakam*) of Guru recites:

"*You are the act of creation, the creator,*
and the myriad variety of what is created;
O God, are you not the very stuff
of which everything is created". [1]

Like the "Cambrian Explosion" – where planetary life forms suddenly multiplied into an amazing variety – the businessman gets the ideation through his ***Entrepreneurial Explosion***". The evolution of the nebulae, the formation of galaxy, the manifestation of the solar system, the accidental formation of planets, the cooling of the crust of the earth...all have happened sequentially as a causal chain of effect. Such a series of inseparable metamorphoses can be seen in the continuation of a business world too. From the microscopic origin to the macroscopic expansion, we can sense a strong "Cause and Effect" relationship: hence, the creative force *Brahama*, the sustaining vitality *Vishnu*, and the final decision maker *Siva* embrace in single reality in an entrepreneur. He is the "***Holy Trinity***" for his business. Hence, in a critical microscopic view, the *Adhyāropa Darśanam* is rightly qualified as *"The Theory of Entrepreneurial Explosion"(or "The Theory of Entrepreneurial Trinity")*.

The sustaining part is more pertinent where *Vishnu* is getting energy from Lakshmi, likening the simile that behind every successful businessman there is a lady; most probably she is his wife.

The number of beads in a kaleidoscope is limited, but the patterns which may arise from the movements of the beads are endless. It is called 'Kaleidoscopic rapidity.' In the same manner, the mind of a promising businessman will weave dream after dream. The dreamer does not doubt anything but remains wake, projects ideas in such a cogent and coherent manner that it should be possible for anyone to gain. Like '*Rishis*' of India, they are existentialists of unlimited sense. They give attention to existence, subsistence, and value.

However, the entrepreneurs hail from Materialist, Spiritualist or semi-semi categories. Whichever be the category they come as *Brahma-Vishnu-Maheswara* roles – they set up business, struggle for sustenance and existence, and accept the destiny, whatever it will be. The brave entrepreneur perceives his latent luminous quality to give out radiant thoughts. The Spiritualists believe that the God created this cosmos with all its myriad varieties. For example, the Gospel, according to St. John, begins: *"In the beginning was the Word, and the Word was with God, and the Word was God... All things were made by Him; and without Him was not anything made... And God said, "Let there be light; and there was light... and God divided the light from the darkness..."*[2]

The Materialists, on the contrary, believe the mythical story in which the Sun gave birth to Space, space then gave birth to Air, air gave birth to Fire, and fire gave birth to Water, and from water came the Earth. Modern science theorizes as an unidentified energy passing through a series of modifications on its way to becoming manifest as this planet. This energy is expressed as nebula, which becomes a star; the explosion of the star forms a planetary system; and finally the cooling of planetary fires allow water and other liquids to condense, leading to the development of an environment and atmosphere conducive to the manifestation of life on the Earth, the planet. Like these stories of evolution, the dormant concepts, incipient memories, visionary ideas, and the psychological urges stockpiled in the consciousness of the magnate entrepreneur explode out and assume objectivity, so that, they become the marvels in the history of business world.

Whichever category – Spiritualists', Materialists', or Semi-Semi – the businessman belongs to, his fundamental convictions may be erroneous as he is a novice in business and his extension of understanding of business realms is limited. For this reason, every chance of business break-down and failure is present. The success rate of business, across the world, is 50 per cent and the reason for 50 per cent failure can be visible in the dark area of fanciful imaginings and beliefs of thalamus of the 'entrepreneur-the-novice.' He is deprived of the languages of transcendence and the metaphysical reality and, hence, his reasoning level is low.

As individuals, we make deliberations and contemplations, and we consider a good number of our decisions to be freely made choices. To clothe an experience in all its richness, we add spices, tastes, and colours with a high degree of sensibility and choose media to popularise it. By doing this, we make our thoughts sophisticated. This sophistication is what is referred to as 'Super-imposition.' It may be called "Applied Psychology." This type of 'cosmic projection' using applied psychology may equate to a mansion built on a shallow bed-rock lacking strength and bearability. And the edifice so built shall face the threat of collapse. Attention deficit and the resultant 'quality-vacuum' may cause headwinds which frighten its survival and longevity. Thus, the 50 per cent start ups get uprooted, as mentioned earlier, basically due to the wrongly indoctrinated convictions.

The failure leads to fear. The modern psychologists identify 'fear with anxiety' out of failure. It may get momentum, too. To surpass it, there must be a 'Guru' for the doers. We can see a '*Guru-paaramparya*' in traditional Vedic culture and religions such as Hinduism, Jainism, Sikhism, and Buddhism. The *Guru-shishya* tradition in *'Mahābhārata'* is vehement. For the trembling and the confused Arjuna, Krishna was more a guru than a charioteer. In the Bhagavad Gita, *Vyasa* gives a symptomatic description of a similar state of *Arjuna* as follows:

" *Oh, Krishna, my limbs fail and my mouth dries up, my body trembles and my hair stands on end. The bow slips from my hand and my skin feels as if burning all over, and I am unable to stand and my mind is whirling round, as it were.* " (Ch.1, v.29,30) [3]

But, Krishna motivates Arjuna:

"Uddhared atmanatmanam,
natmanam avasadayet,
atmaiva hy atmano bandhur,
atmaiva ripur atmanah. " (Bhagavad Gita, 6.5: Sankhya Yoga).[4]

Meaning, "*A man must elevate himself by his own mind, not degrade himself. The mind is the friend of the conditioned soul, and his enemy as well.* "

The mind that realises its true nature is a pure mind. A conditioned mind is obstructive, empirically and esoterically. Inhibitive negative latencies do give in to righteous conduct for effective redressal.

Adhyāropa Darśanam, in sum and substance, is the exercise of *IDEATION*. In this exercise, the business man, especially a novice, may super-impose his dreamlike, myth-making fantasies, and may indulge in the actualisation of latent potentials favoured by ignorance and passion. He may, later, realise the fallacies slowly, and may apply the philosophical pursuits to reclaim and re-establish truth. Then only he will understand that the snake he has visualised in a piece of coir is not snake but it is a piece of coir only.

The intention of the first *Darśana* is to reveal and to make known that the initial fault-cum-immature steps taken by Start-ups and the struggles for survival by their promoters in the formative periods. Inevitably there come the accusations, superimpositions, mud-slinging, and passing the bucks, as beautifully expressed by Stephen B. Maurer: *"Hen A pecks B, B pecks C, and C pecks D…"*[5]

In fine, Adhyāropa means the super-imposition or wrong projection of the qualities or properties of one thing on another. It is the cosmic projection of qualities and attributes of one thing/person/object upon others without knowing whether it is correct or incorrect. Similarly, at the beginning, the much enthused entrepreneur goes leads and bounds, create chaos, do exploitation, pollution and get anchored at wrong harbour. In the hectic paths of business-running, the entrepreneur slips from the civic conditions, challenging laws, out-stepping boundaries, and scales the fragile heights of business management, neglecting the very law of the land even. At this stage, the business may have been ideated and sprouted only and in its growth path it is remaining at its very rudimentary stage which may be named **"Pre-Traditional Society."** Nevertheless, it is not the healthy way of running a business at all. The de-railed promoters must get re-railed. Here we see the importance of the next vision, *Apavāda Darśanam.*

[Recapitulation: (IDEATION) The owner of a business is the *Brahma, Vishnu, and Maheswara* of his business. The business idea cannot be super-imposed; rather it shall be a spontaneous overflow of powerful thoughts recollected from a protracted and designed action. The so-called ideas of ready-made nature will be liability. Only a well-thought-out idea, based on a thorough market study, would materialise. A learned Guru is a guide here]

Adhyāropa Darśanam

1. Guru Nitya Chaitanya Yati, (1981), *"The English translation of Daiva Dasakam",* verse 5, 1st edition, Mangala Press, Varkala, Kerala.

2. *The Bible*, John, 1:1–5.

3. *Bhagavad Gita*, Ch.1, v. 29–30.

4. *Bhagavad Gita*, 6.5: Sankhya Yoga.

5. Maurer, S.B., (March 2, 1980), *"The King Chicken Theorems,"* Mathematics Magazine, Mathematical Association of America, the USA.

Chapter 2

APAVĀDA DARŚANAM

Meaning:

> *APAVĀDA* is the anti-dote for *ADHYĀROPA*. When the qualities or properties of one thing are wrongly projected or superimposed on another, it is called *ADHYĀROPA* and the systematic method of correcting a false notion is called *APAVĀDA*. Thus *APAVĀDA* is a philosophical method used to re-calm and re-establish truth. It is a method with which we can eradicate all false identifications from our minds.

The World is "Subtle" and "Gross" and it contains everything in uniform. The Lord Himself is the "subject matter" and the "object matter" of the Universe. Apart from Him, nothing is there. He is the "cause" and He is the "effect." Apart from cause there is no effect.

'He' is Absolute. He created the Universe in its "subtle" ("*suksma*") and "gross" ("*Sthūla*") forms. This World, which is of gross and subtle forms, comes from consciousness; if it is affirmed, everything is existence through and through and if it is denied, it is consciousness through and through. Therefore, all this is unreal. For the unreal, how can there be origin? How can there be dissolution? That which has no origin or no dissolution is none other than the Supreme Absolute.

Through *MĀYĀ* only the confusion arises that there is origin and there is dissolution.

Because of the non-difference from cause, how can an effect come to have existence? And how can there be the non-existence of cause too?

The Absolute alone is real. When all parts are separated one by one, then one sees everything as conscious alone. Dividing all parts one by one, everything is seen there. "What is truly existent" vs "What is merely fanciful imagery" take us to the "world of transactions" and to the "world of dreams (illusions)". From a piece of cloth, the threads can be pulled out, one after another, until no cloth remains. Now the thread itself can be untwisted and unwound until only a heap of cotton fibre is left. Every fibre can then be de-structured until the heap of the fibre is no more. In the laboratory, the constituents of the fibre can be separated and revealed. When this is done, the same 'cotton' is no longer applicable.

Thus, it is the "pure mind stuff" that sees the world in its "gross" and "subtle" versions. The world of transactions called 'objective reality', and the world of dream called 'subjective illusion' are the two levels of understanding. The former is the understanding of what is truly in existence and the later is the merely fanciful imagery of the mind.

Consciousness alone shines; there is nothing other than consciousness. And what does not shine is unreal and the unreal does not shine. Human beings must withdraw from the world of ignorance. The redemption from the clutches of ignorance will promote us to the positive path of ascending the mount of eternal bliss.

Management Concepts of *Apavāda Darśanam*

[VISION OF TRUTH]

(The Ability to Imbibe Truth by Consistent Refutation of the False)

> *"I have not failed. I have just found 10,000 ways that won't work."*
>
> **– Thomas Alva Edison**

Apavāda Darśanam is 'Vision of Truth.' It can also be named as 'Vision of Non-Supposition.'

This Universe is "Subtle" and "Gross". It contains everything in uniform, but not in different types. It is you, the businessman, to safeguard and shape it according to your choice. The "cause" and "effect" are not different and two, but they are one. No cause, no effect. If one does not do, there is no meaning in mere thinking about it. If you think, you must do. Doing brings it into existence; otherwise it will remain as a part of the ultimate Absolute.

All the successful business personalities in the world – Apple, Face Book, Google... are doers. They are the "pure mind stuffs", and they shine among others. The "pure mind" means "VISION". Only a 'Visionary' can shine. He sees the *Sūksma – Sthūla* versions. 'Vision' means the stuff of 'high value'. It is the divine bliss. The one who is visionary and having the stuff of 'high value' will exist, subsist, and shine. Others will doom into failure.

A spiritual believer wants to prove that the **'Self'** is the only reality and he will see everything as a manifestation of the **'Self'** and he becomes a lover of the manifested world. But, for the materialists, what is important is 'Matter'. This same matter, in its most elaborate and complex form, is the totality of nature. And they believe that all sentient beings are part of nature and can be persuaded of their essential sameness and will be possible to establish the ideal classless society. In such a world, humanity as a class would be considered as one and the same entity. For them, the growth and development are the processes of evolution.

Unfortunately, the prejudices between the two factions cannot be eradicated. *Apavāda* is an effective method that we can use for this purpose. It addresses both – the prejudices arising from misguided spiritual enthusiasms and the prejudices stemming from the slogan-mongering exaggerations of materialism.

But how?

Yes, by 'Gross-Subtle Analysis.'

Then, what is Gross and what is Subtle?

The Sanskrit term for Gross is '*Sthūla*' and for Subtle is '*Suksma.*' *["Suksma" is that kind of awareness and comprehension arrived at by relating concepts which exist as ideas in the mind, without much reference to the presence of objective data; "Sthūla" is that kind of knowledge which is structured with impressions derived from our sensory system viz., form, colour, physical dimension, weight and so on].*

The **Sthūla-Sūksma Analysis** may be called a **Joint-and-Several Analysis.** It can also be called a **Macro-Micro Analysis.** A comprehensive analysis of *Sthūla-Sūksma* aspects would render a rather reliable result. Guru says: **"Chaitanyad agatam Sthūla-Suksmatmakam idam jagat',** means the Gross-Subtle Analysis brings Consciousness (prowess) in the world. It ensures a **'J-turn'** manoeuvre for business and to speed up its journey forward in correct direction.

Apavāda Darśanam is an extension of understanding to the fundamental convictions. Spiritualists or materialists, both sides want to learn truth. A systematic method of correcting a false notion is, in Sanskrit, called *Apavāda*. And it can be called the *"Sthūla – Sūksma* Model" of Narayana Guru. It is, in essence, the renowned **"Five Why (5Y) Analysis"** developed by Sakichi Toyoda,[1] to explore the cause-and-effect relationships underlying a particular problem. The primary goal of the technique is to determine the root cause of a defect or problem by repeating the question "Why." Each answer forms the basis of the next question. By repeating 'Why' five times, the nature of the problem as well as its solution becomes apparent. Thus the *Sthūla-Sūksma* Analysis of Guru is the **Root Cause Analysis,** and hence, *Apavāda Darśanam* can be rightly defined as *"The Theory of Gross-Subtle (Sthūla Suksma) Analysis" (or "The Theory of Root Cause Analysis").*

In a closed definition, the '*Stula-Sūksma* Analysis' reaches in, in sum and substance, the **Six Sigma (6σ)** technique introduced by Bill Smith at Motorola in 1980. [2] What did Jack Welch at General Electric in 1995 [3] was its still advanced version. Six Sigma is a disciplined, statistical-based, data-driven procedure for "Continuous Improvement." It is a methodology for eliminating defects in a product, process, or service in its production and distribution.

The *Sthūla-Sūksma Analysis* of Sree Narayana Guru reverberates in the modern Japanese Ideologies of *Kaizen* and *Kanban.*

The Japanese word 'Kaizen' stands for **"Change for Better."**[4.] It aims at a "Continuous Betterment Through Change." Briefly, it is Change Management." The story of the kaizen miracle was introduced in Toyota Company in the 1930s by its founder Sakichi Toyota with a slogan: **"Open the window; it is a big**

world out there." And in 1950 Toyota implemented **"Quality Circles"** which led to the development of Toyota's unique **"Toyota Production System"** which focussed on "continuous improvement in quality, technology, processes, company culture, productivity, safety and leadership." In turn it assured the "faster delivery, lower costs, and greater custom satisfaction, nay, customer delight." And Masaaki Imai introduced the Kaizen to the Western world in 1986 which spread across the world soon. Look through any angle, the sum and substance of kaizen is the *Sthūla-Sūksma* **Philosophy."**

The Japanese production technique *"Kanban"*[5] developed by the Engineer-businessman, Taiichi Ohno, for Toyota, is a methodology to fix the potential bottlenecks and hindrances in the production processes and work-flows and address them properly so that there is a smooth work flow. It is a planning system aiming at control and management of work and inventory at every stage of production so as to assure optimum productivity. It is a visionary gift emanate from *Sthūla-Sūksma* exercise.

A businessman must be both a spiritualist and a materialist. He must be a distinguisher of "Science" (Knowledge) and "Ne-science" (Ignorance). "When self-knowledge shrinks, then ignorance looms large and a rope becomes a serpent, a shadow becomes a ghost. **"It is the effect of 'Ne-science' (ignorance) where the truth hides in oblivion"**, says Guru.

Apavāda Darsana stands for the clear knowledge of the 'Self'. One must realise the negative nature of ignorance and the positive aspect of wisdom. Non-righteousness is born of ignorance and it ends up in spiritual darkness. Spiritual awareness makes life easier as our faculties become illuminated and wisdom prevails. *"A little leaven leaveneth the whole* lump*".* [6]

The businessman must be a 'Visionary' to undergo *Sthūla-Sūksma* Analysis to shine and upgrade himself. As an ordinary man he is suffering from the 'Three Great Ignorances: one, 'Insecurity on the Earth'; two, 'Extremities of the Nature'; and three, 'His own Ego and Blind-foldingness.' Let him be conscious, realise the 'Gross-Subtle' aspects, and do recognise the *Yin* and *Yang* of everything. He must realise the difference between the 'Objective Reality' and the 'Subjective Illusion.' He is the man who realises the 'emptiness and ridiculousness' of the world-game, and the fake castles upheld by 'MĀYĀ', deviated from the strait path of wisdom.

The tortuous paths of *Māyā* are dangerous. The opening statement of the Holy Qur'an is a prayer to Allah to lead the worshiper safely through the tortuous path of *Māyā:*

> *"In the name of Allah, the Beneficent, the Merciful,*
> *praise be to Allah, Lord of the Worlds,*
> *The Beneficent, the Merciful,*
> *Owner of the Day of judgement,*
> *Thee (alone) we worship; Thee (alone) we ask for help,*
> *Show us the straight path,*
> *The path of those whom Thou hast favoured;*
> *Not (the path) of those who earn Thine anger nor of those*
> *who go astray."*[7]

In the *Arthashastra*, Chanakya says, "*Dharmasya Moolam Arthah*", means, "Prosperity is the Root of Righteousness."[8] Agreed. The wick has to be immersed (partially) in the oil for the lamp to burn. But, If the wick is completely drowned in the oil, it cannot bring light. Life is like the wick of the lamp. If one is drowned in the materialism of the world, he cannot bring joy and knowledge in his life. So, better it is to be Materialist-cum-Spiritualist. If it comes so, Guru would be right of advising **"Arthah Moolam Dharmasya"**, means the "Root of Prosperity is Righteousness." It is the Guru's 'righteous' path. It emphasises the Gandhian philosophy of **"both the ends and means must be justifiable."**

World across, the success rate of business, on an average is 50 per cent. In India also, the statistics says so. It is often said that more than half of new businesses disappear during the first year itself. According to the Small Business Administration(SBA),[9] 30 per cent of new small businesses fail during the first two years of being open; 50 per cent during the first five years; and 66 per cent during the first 10 years. Why it so happens? It just so happens, in a general parlance, that the Entrepreneurs lack planning, lack effective time-management, and lack persistence. The majority of individuals rush headfirst into entrepreneurship, and the resultant economic upheaval, with the enthusiasm and zeal of a kid in a candy store. The financial, emotional, mental, and subsequent spiritual drain can be enough to send even the most astute individuals running for rope. But for the *Sthūla-Sūksma Nireekshan*, they go astray. Had they ever gone through "Michael Porter's Five Forces Model (5F)",[10] or "Albert Humphrey's SWOT Analysis"[11] "For Business Planning", the failure could have been averted or at least minimised. Had they ever touched the "DO, Decide, Delegate, Delete" – the Eisenhower Method for Time Management – as a tutorial "For Effective Time Management', the business could have been rescued. Had they ever experienced "Entrepreneurship" according to Peter Drucker",[12] "For Persistence In Running Business" (Peter Drucker Theories), the dip and slip could have been kept at bay. Let alone Sree Narayana Guru's *"Sthūla-Sūksma Nireekshan."*

However, by now the business has reached to its second level of growth, say, *"The Traditional Society"*, with a little progress.

[Recapitulation: (VISIONARY) A business man must be a Visionary; he must know the truth; he must fight ne-science and install wisdom in himself. He must have the knowledge of the "Sthūla-Sūksma Model" of Narayana Guru]

Apavāda Darśanam

1. Sakichi Toyoda, the Japanese Industrialist, inventor and founder of Toyota Industries, (1930), *"5 Whys technique"* *(5 Whys Analysis)*.

2. Smith, Bill., American Engineer working at Motorola, (1980), *"Six Sigma Techniques."*

3. Jack Welch Jr, John Francis., American Business Executive, author, and chemical engineer, and CEO of General Electric 1981–2001, (1995), applied *"Six sigma"* in General Electric, America.

4. Masaaki Imai, (1986), *"Kaizen: The key to Japan's Competitive Success."*

5. Taiichi Ohno, (1940s), Toyota, Japan.

6. *The Bible*, Corinthians 5:6.

7. *The Holy Qur'an,* A Yusuf Ali (trans.), American Trust Publications, p.14.

8. Chanakya Sutra, *"the second sutra,"* (of the first ten prominent sutras of total 572 sutras), *echanakya. blogspot.com.*

9. Small Business Administration (SBA), USA, www.sba.gov.

10. Porter, Michael Eugene, American Academic, Professor at Harvard Business School, (1979), *"Five Forces Analysis"*, Harvard Business Review.

11. Humphrye, Albert S., American Business Theorist, and Management Consultant, (1960s), *"SWOT Analysis" (Strengths, Weaknesses, Opportunities, Threats),* a research Project at Stanford University, California, USA, in the 1960s and 1970s.

12. Drucker, Peter Ferdinand, Austrian-born American Management Consultant, educator, and author, (1909–2005), *"Management Theories."*

Chapter 3

ASATHYA DARŚANAM

Meaning:

There are "Darkness" ("*Tamas*") and "Ignorance", ("*Avidya*"). All are a permeation of mind but mind is invisible, in the same way, as the blue in the sky. By ignorance, which is none other than the mind, all worlds are imagined, then everything becomes like a painting. The darkness comes in the forms of lust, greed, suspicion, hatred, or attachment. Each of these brands of darkness has its own promptings and compositions of mental images.

The visible is imagined by the will; the visible is seen only where there is will. Where there is no will, the rope may be misrepresented as snake. The 'myth-making faculty' of man returns home in the dark and man is afraid of the "other". Ghosts and goblins have only nominal existence in the world of semantics. Yet the myth-making faculty of the mind of man fabricates images of different colours.

The fear of non-existent entities arises because of 'Ne-science' ('Ignorance'). As a remedy there is *"Atmavidya"* ("knowledge of the *Atma* or Self}. It is a discipline of understanding evolved by seers over a period of thousands of years, and they have found it to be effective in releasing individuals from the negative conditions arising from 'Ignorance'. By ignorance, all worlds are imagined as a good painting. Like a ghost to a coward in the darkness, the imagination becomes unreal objects. It is not truth. The mind is ignorant, in darkness, and a wonder like *Indra's* magic. Everything, like *Indra's* magic, seems to be real by superimposition. *Māyā* alone is the primal cause of the world, and *Māyā* creates everything. One, who reasons correctly, then appears to him as a mirage, otherwise, by confusion, things seem real. To the mature mind, the world appears as a forest in the sky.

There are three sources of ignorance. To be clearer, there are three kinds of pains to which human beings are exposed to. **First,** the 'insecurity in our life on the Earth', which is ruled by universal laws, and we are at a loss to comprehend the functional secrets of these laws. At this stage, man turns to the 'Unknown', a supernatural being or the so-called God, with prayers of supplication and seeks its (His) succour. This is the field which eludes man's comprehension and it is called *'aadhidaivikam'*.

Second, human beings are challenged by the 'extremities of nature'. We, for our sustenance, have to depend upon the nature – the earth and the sea – and in all such endeavours we have to tame the nature. But, the nature does not change her laws, so that, man has to be in harmony with it. Here, man develops many devices to make nature more habitable and lovable. This is the field of empirical transactions and it is called *'aadhibhactikam'*.

Third, 'the misery of man is man himself'. No one is a greater enemy to man than his own self. The 'ego and prejudices of all sorts' that he rears form an axis against himself and acts against any sensible transactions with his fellow beings. The multifarious ills of the body and mind are all created by own ignorance and darkness. Ultimately, always and everywhere, he is confined to the problems perpetuated by him and other members of the society. This field in which man struggles and fears is called **'aadhimaanusikam'**.

This ignorance can, collectively, be called *'avidya'*. The Guru advises a withdrawal from the world of ignorance (*avidya*). When we light a lamp in a room, the light is of one light and when we light a thousand lamps, the whole room will be flooded with light. This means that light and darkness remain close together in a physical sense. Similarly, a mind can have bright thoughts and can also be surrounded by monstrous and demonic moods, attitudes, and intentions. Through *'Atmavidya'*, we can remove these dark spots and can attain the 'eidetic' awareness.

Management Concepts of *Asathya Darśanam*

[VISION OF NON-EXISTENCE]

(The Ability to Realise the Reality or Self and the Ability to Discern the Real from the Un-real)

"Wisdom out-weights any wealth."

– Sophocles

It is the 'Vision of Non-existence.'

Means?

It means simple that what we see is not existing and real; rather it is all unreal and only the permeation of our 'mind.' And this 'Vision' is, hence, mainly to focus our attention on sifting the unreal from the real.

For many people, reality is what they see. Pain and pleasure, fact and fiction, transiency and persistence etc., are all not reality but only consciousness of man. All these phenomena come in active form when we are awake; when we are in deep sleep, such phenomena do not manifest. In a nutshell, what we call reality is really not real but a 'pseudo reality.'

Everything perceived and conceived is basically the manifestation one's own consciousness. What we actually experience is the result of a kaleidoscopic shake-up of the psychological structure. In fact, the blue colour of the sky is to be seen more in the bio-chemical function of the brain. The light reaches retina of the eye transforms in to electrical impulses, passes through the neurons of the brain, which subjects to various bio-chemical permutations and the resultant psychological response to the incoming sensory data produces the experience of seeing the blue sky. The astronauts who have gone into outer space have experience only utter darkness and not anything blue. The blue sky is only a collective hallucinatory projection which Guru calls **'Viksepa.'**

We live mostly in a fantasized world of values generated by the mind, so that, it is not clear about what is true and what is untrue, what is real and what is unreal, and what is worthy and what is un-worthy. If it so happens that the mind is creating one fantasy after another, and goes unbridled, we will land in a fantasy world. This tendency of mind to breed false values into its own fantasy is described as *'Avidya,'* the ignorance. This ignorance (*avidya*) and the consequential darkness (*tamas*) are the chief reasons for business failiures as discussed in the previous chapter.

The panacea to fight against this *avidya* is *'atmavidya,'* says Guru. *Atmavidya* means knowledge of *'atma'* or 'Self.' This darkness and *avidya* – *'tamas'* and *'avidya'* respectively – will place us on a "darkling plain", as sung by Mattew Arnold, the Victorian writer.[1] So, one must know the Self. By knowing the Self, one becomes truth. The Nature is fecund and its possibilities are endless. In the everlasting march of the Nature, one must see the truth and must realise the real from the unreal. The mature person does that; he is wise and there arises a natural consciousness out of the subjective promptings. Then the duality fades out, the blissful nature of the Self slowly or suddenly becomes unveiled and wisdom prevails.

An ignorant mind sacrifices his health, time and talents for the realisation of his private ends created by his ignorant mind. He engages in skepticism, myth-making, fantasising of forms and situations, spinning of stories, and in disjunctive thoughts. These negatives produce many forms of irrational fear and doubts and he may even go insane. The total pathological rhythm is affected and a sense of insecurity and fear germinate. Thereafter there is no run. When the businessman becomes sick of insecurity and fear, the business will fall into the quagmire of failure.

On the other hand, when individual minds get operated in a corporate whole, for the benefit of the universal mankind, it is called 'Universal Projection.' It is a sacrifice to the Absolute and emphasising a 'Universal Value' in preference for the transient pleasures of the world. As a result, the individual becomes unified with the Absolute. When one promotes himself to this level of understanding, it is called 'Self-realisation.' And the Self-realisation is the product of *atmavidya*. In fine, it is the "Theory of *Atmavidya*" of Narayana Guru is the ever alchemy of the 'Universal Understanding and Brotherhood.' The emergence of this awareness, its meaningful persistence, and the interaction of subject and object with it, can be equated to what the modern psychologists call a 'Gestalt.'. The core of the 'theory of Gestalt' emphasises that the whole of anything is greater than the sum of its parts. What is pertinent in the corporate world is this Gestalt. It is the unifying force which fights against disintegration and promises *esprit de corps* in the Organisation. This is the power of *atmavidya*. And *Asathya Darśanam* can be defined vividly as *"The Theory of Atmavidya" (or "The Theory of Self Knowledge")*.

The 'Theory of *Atmavidya*' is tested through the simile of "rope-the-snake."The mode of operation of ignorance whereby a piece of rope is mistaken for a snake in the twilight is the essence of it. Guru says, for such a misapprehension, there should be four factors: firs,the person's fear of snake; second, the previously formulated image of snake; third, lack of proper light, and fourth, a piece of rope which is somewhat similar in size and shape of a snake. In the simile, only the piece of rope has existential verity. The prevalence of darkness creates an ideal situation for the projection of a presentiment. The presentiment is a previously acquired image associated with fear. The whole coloration of the situation is derived from fear and ignorance of mind. If the element of darkness and fear disappear, the snake also vanishes. Such is the case of 'shadow-the-ghost.' In the absence of light, the shadow of anything will be mistaken as ghost or goblin.

So, get the fear and ignorance discarded, and develop faith and courage, instead. Guru teaches that through *atmavidya*, we can develop *prajna*, the mass of consciousness. In sum and substance it is Self-Awareness. Thus, *Asathya Darśanam* advocates nothing else but 'Self Awareness.'

Where there is fear, there emerges insecurity. The fear and insecurity are the by-products of ignorance and nescience. All these do contribute to folklores and misbelieves. There is no boundary for such delusions. Mr. Geoffrey Hodson, of the Theosophical Society of India, has published a beautifully illustrated book describing his encounters with hundreds of *Devas* and *Nature Spirits*.[2] America has its legends of beings such as 'Big Foot', while in the Himalayan Folklore the abominable 'Snow Man' (Yeti) emerges. The digital number 13 is considered to be inauspicious in many western Countries. Witches and vampires loom large in Shakespearean dramas…

Asathya Darśanam directs entrepreneurs that fear is a deep-seated ignorance or conditioning, and it can be rectified only by reclaiming the 'Self' from the vicissitudes of ignorance.

The Upanishad theory of *"Hita"* focuses on casting out fear. The "Bright" and "Dark" forces (*"Taijasi"* and *"Tamasi"*) are equally forceful like *Yin* and *Yang*. The Winners who achieve material status are playing this **"POSITIVE"** mind stuff. If truth is hidden and untruth is veiling it, one can never reach the truth without first removing the veil of this ignorance. What we need here is a "strong will". Defence, sports, politics, business, education...wherever and whatever it would be, what is relevant and inevitable is this strong will and faith. *"And He said to them...if you have faith the size of a mustard seed, you will say to the mountain, 'Move from here to there', and it will move, and nothing will be impossible for you."* (Matthew 17:20)[3] For 'strong mind stuff', there is no-ending, and it warrants vast, 'Blue Sky' for start, sustenance, and growth. Even the vast blue serenity of the sky is not the limit for such people who turn their *tamas* to *rajas* and *rajas* to *satva* by *Atmavidya*. Both the Cosmic Science and Consciousness Science come to their reach. This can be coined as *"**Blue Sky Strategy**"* like the "Blue Ocean Strategy" of W. Chan Kim and Renee Mauborgue.[4] Blue Sky Strategy may also be named as **'Blue Sky Leadership'** (**'Blue Sky Insider' or 'Blue Sky Shift'**).

Asathya Darśanam, in essence, reveals the intrinsic insight of "Johari Window"[5] to business community. The darker and blacker the intellect, despite strength and capability of the body, there is no realisation. Lighting the lamp of *dhyana* and *Jñāna* and to illuminate the body, mind, and soul and seek inner virtues for the good of self and the society is the philosophical reference of Johari Window Model for improving 'Self-Awareness and team work', developed by American Psychologists – Joseph Luft and Harry Ingham. *"Light gives of itself freely filling all available space. It does not seek anything in return; it asks not whether you are friend or foe. It gives of itself and is not thereby diminished"* – Michael Strassfeld.[6]

In a true analytical sense, *Asathya Darśanam* proposes an **"Inner Engineering"** via *Atmavidya* advised by the Guru. Through *atmavidya* (knowledge of Self) one wards off the fears and doubts and attains a divine light to fight against *avidya* the ignorance and builds Self-esteem and confidence to rise up. The promoter of the business sees the vast-high blue sky to fly and reach. It is the third stage of growth, say, **Pre-Pre-Conditions for Take Off**. Now a clear trail of growth is visible for the business.

[Recapitulation: (INNER ENGINEERING) The businessman must be a man of Self awareness, Courage and Wisdom. He must be a man of will and Faith. Theory of *Atmavidya* is his success mantra]

Asatya Darśanam

1. Arnold, Matthew., English Poet, (1822 – 1888), *"Dover Beach,"* last three lines.

2. Hodson, Geoffrey.,(2003), *"The Fairy Kingdom,"* Book Tree Publications, amazon.com

3. *Holy Bible*, 'Faith Moving Mountains', Matthew 17:20

4. W. Chan Kim and Renee Mauborgue (2004), *"Blue Ocean Strategy : How to Create Uncontested Market Space and Make the Competition Irrelevant"*, Harward Business Review Press.

5. Luft, J.,and Ingham, H (1961), *"The Johari Window: a graphic model of awareness in interpersonal relations,"* 5 (9), p.6–7.

6. Michael Strassfeld, Rabbi Emeritus., (2002), *"A Book of Life: Embracing Judaism as a Spiritual Practice,"* Schocken Books, New York, USA.

Chapter 4

MĀYĀ DARŚANAM

Meaning:

The Sphere of human experience is divided into two – 'conscious' and 'unconscious'. The 'conscious' covers the large experiences like sensations, feelings, fantasies, dreams, passive observation, critical observation, active reasoning, conscious volition, various kinds of conflicts etc., which are expressed at the level of awareness. The 'unconscious' is operational in a very much wider field, having unfathomable depth that is not reachable to normal human awareness. What occurs in the conscious sphere of mind and its experiences are the indicators of the causal factors lying hidden in the depths of the conscious sphere.

What is not known is *Māyā*. It tells us that what is dormant and hidden in unfathomable chasm of unconscious mind has its ebbs and flows in the upper periphery of conscious mind. The negative factors conceal truth from us. We fail to segregate real from the unreal.

We are motivated by *Māyā* and veiled by our ignorance. If we put a strait rod or stick into a glass half filled with water, the part of the rod/stick in the water will be seen as slightly bent. When we pull it out of the water, it looks straight again. By comparing the two states, we come to know of the fallacy of vision. It is due to refraction. In the same manner, *Māyā* is to be treated as a refractive index of the degree of deviation in the erroneous transaction of life. Like a tree in a seed, exists the *Māyā*, the marvel. One who wins is the one who recognises this *Māyā*.

Like the clay in a pot, only the Absolute is real and known. The Self is vidya and it recognises the truth about rope and snake. When the Self is unreal and Non-self is real, it is *Avidya* and it says a rope a snake. The 'reasoning Self' can easily recognise *Māyā*. The senses are the imagery of the gross, and the senses, mind, and intelligence assist the exercise of reasoning the Self. By ignorance we say the mother-of-pearl is silver. It is *tamas*. It is dark. It is nescience. A tree is wonderfully hidden in a seed. But, it sprouts and get diversified when the situations favour.

The five senses, the mind, the intelligence, and other vital tendencies are the creations of the self. So, the Self is Atman. Only the Atman is true. All others are *Māyā* in life. The superimposition of falsehood is prevailing everywhere. Atman means the Self. One who recognises the power and potency of the Self will succeed. The knowledge of the Self is '*suddha Jñānam*' and it is the pursuit of success.

Management Concepts of *Māyā Darśanam*

[VISION OF NEGATION]

(The Ability to Pre-suppose the existence of whatever is referred to)

> *"Innovation distinguishes between a leader and a follower."*
>
> **– Steve Jobs**

Māyā **Darśanam** is 'Vision of Negation. It can also be qualified as 'Vision of Non-being Beingness.' It is a critical study of both the 'noumenon and the phenomenon'.

Guru gives us directions, and we can use the directions to enable us to discern the faithful basis of superimpositions of falsehood. Guru helps us to recognise and extract the real from the unreal and helps us to have a correct perception of the empirical world and its transactional variety. Further, Guru reveals the negative factors which obscure and hide truth from us.

The Self is the basis of the world. It is the mother-of-pearl. It is the basis of the silver-presentiment. It removes darkness. Like a tree in a seed, the *MĀYĀ* exists. Same is the case of the 'prime potent power' in you. One who recognises the power and potency alone will succeed. Self is Atman; negative self-will err and fail; the positive self is potency and will correct and survive.

The miraculous operations of our own psycho-physical systems is the essence of the unknown functional intelligence – body-building, respiration, blood circulation, digestion of food, and elimination of waste. The power of mind to know such hidden aspects warrants a pure knowledge called *'suddha Jñānam'*.

The four main causes of any effect, in Aristotelian logic, are the material cause, efficient cause, instrumental cause, and final cause. For example., the material used in the manufacture of a pot is clay (material cause), the intentionality of the potter and his craftsmanship in making a pot (efficient cause), the required instruments like potter's wheel, kiln etc., (instrumental cause), and the water, fuel, and the assembling of the ingredients etc., (final cause). The poet who writes a poem, the artist who paints a picture, a sculptor who carves a sculpture, a playwright who produces a drama, an entrepreneur who runs a business – all begin their role at the negative alpha pole of consciousness. They all distinguish between right knowledge and fallacious perception – the factual and the fictitious.

To apprehend the real, one has to transcend the transactional. The transactional world is unreal. A true leader is one who is transcending, not transactional, in nature. Ignorance is the world of transactions. The world of transactions is also the world of action, and action creates reactions. So, our lives are simply filled with the chains of actions and reactions. Attachment, bondage, rivalry, competitions – all these are present actively in the world of transactions. But, a transcendental leader applies wisdom without neglecting his role on the world of transactions. '*Isavasya Upanishad*' speaks of such a man. He is saved from the transient values of transactional world. The best examples of the application of wisdom in transactional life can be seen in the life-styles of Buddha and Lao Tzu – the immortals of wisdom.

A successful leader is a Transcendental Leader. A 'transactional leader' goes for the 'actual' (*yathartha*), but, the 'Transcendental leader' seeks the 'real' (*paramartha).* An efficient method for the discernment of the Real from the Unreal is wisdom. The false identity of the 'I-consciousness' finds no place in the realm of wisdom. The transcendental leader would be reflective, value-centred, global in perspective, and a facilitator of dialog. Transcendent leadership provides a revolutionary frame of viewing human interactions in organisational settings. As the society is shifting from old to new paradigms, we are gradually progressing towards transcendental leadership from transactional leadership.

As the Biblical adage goes *"A little leaven leaveneth the whole lump"*, a little wisdom can transform one's life completely positive. The number of beads in a kaleidoscope is limited, but the patterns which may arise from the movements of the beads are endless. Similarly, the creative genius of man is lying dormant in business minds; the depth is the domain where *"tamas"* (darkness) envelops his consciousness; in that state the *'satva'* (the idea) is cut off from opportunities to come in contact with external things (forces) and remains passive. This passive sleeping state is called *'sushupti'* (deep sleep) and like a sperm imprisoned in a seed for an opportunity to come up. The opportunity or the reason to activate the sperm is, *'kaarana' (the cause)*, says Guru. The *satva* (the idea) is knocked down by *tamas* (darkness) and assumes *sushupti* (deep sleep) finds *Kaarana* (the cause) via the critical study of Noumenon and Phenomenon, so that, results *kaarya* (the effect). Where the *satva* is awakened from *sushupti* by *kaarana* sidelining *tamas* and *avidya,* so that, results *kaarya,* there is the normal success path of Transcendental Leadership.

Guru warns that *'Māyā'* (*avidya*) operates as a negative potential force even at the level of transcendence. *'Māyā'* has the power to take us to the sublimity (greatness/nobility) of transcendental heights, and also to bog down to the individuated consciousness with all its wretchedness. The Semitic religions use a hateful 'Satanic' principle, which counteracts the benevolence of God, and this negative force is nothing else but *'Māyā'* – the ne-science. The seat of *Māyā* is subconscious mind. *Māyā* is very powerful; as powerful as *Asuras*. If one could realise *Māyā* and convert its negative potential to positive force, he becomes a transcendental leader. One who outwits subconscious mind and *Māyā* and one who transforms negative potential to positive force, and one who transcends from transactional character to transcendental traits, would win in his endeavours. Only the leader who can distinguish between Noumenon and Phenomenon and the one who can segregate the *Real* from the *Māyā* can reach to this level of leadership. So, *Māyā Darśanam* can be called **"The Theory of Noumenon and phenomenon" (or "The Theory of Nescience and Science").**

Krishna advises Arjuna not to bemoan anything of a transient nature (*Māyā*), and everything except the 'Transcendent Absolute'. Guru, in his **Universal Prayer (*Daiva Dasakam*)**, recites:

"As ocean, wave, wind, and depth,
Let us within see the scheme
of us, nescience,
your glory and you."[1]

"Are you not Māyā, the wielder of Māyā,
and also the rejoicer in Māyā?
Are you not the True One who,
having removed Māyā, grants the Supreme Union?"[2]

Guru goes further ahead – from transcendent (*para*) to "Immanence" (*apāra*). Only God is "Immanent" (*apāra*). Immanent Leadership is the "Leadership of Transcendent Absolute."

Has anybody, ever heard of Immanent Leadership? Who is an Immanent Leader? What are the traits of such a Leader? Any Immanent Leader present anywhere in the world? Many a questions emerge. But answers...? Nil. Perhaps, Lord Krishna might be one. How did He do in *Kurukshetra* might be the length and breadth of Immanent Leadership. It is *apāra... param apāra*. It is *param param apāra*. (The author does not know whether there are phrases like "*param apāra*" and "*param param apāra*" in Sanskrit or not). Any number of superlatives could fail to qualify the attributes of "Immanent Leadership" propounded by Guru.

Anyhow, to make it at least comprehensive, an **Immanent Leader** is one who permanently pervades and sustains the Universe. It is the pervasive, pervading, and permeating leadership. It is suffusive and omnipresent and ubiquitous in nature. In fine it is "Godly Leadership." This Godly/Immanent Leadership can be only imaginary and is impossible to be seen in reality. So, we are limiting our approach to *"The Theory of Noumenon and Phenomenon"* for better, than thinking about *"The Theory of Immanent Leadership."*

How did Guru propose such a concept which is beyond comprehension? What Age or which century people shall enjoy the marvels of such a leadership? Or will it remain as stranger than fiction forever? Perhaps, such fathomless thoughts might be the reasons why Guru's *Darśana Mālā* is qualified as *"Bhagavad-Gita-The-Second"* *(Bhagavad Gita 2.0)*.

[Recapitulation: (IMMANENT LEADERSHIP) POSITIVE SELF, POSITIVE THOUGHTS, AND POSSIBILITY THOUGHTS of Businessman find the Prime Potent Power for a transcendental paradigm so as to aim at Immanent Leadership]

Māyā Darśanam

1. Sree Narayana Guru, (1914), *"Daiva Dasakam,"* verse 4, prayer penned by Sree Narayana Guru circa 1914.

2. ibid. verse 6.

Chapter 5

BHĀNA DARŚANAM

Meaning:

The mind is capable of feeling, reasoning and willing. Man has a physical body equipped with sensory organs and a mind. The mind that reasons, the senses that perceive, and the organs that act – these are estimated by consciousness. Each of these faculties has its own field of experience – like the sun shines, the wind blows, and the cloud rains. Nature exists and functions as a whole. In it is no categorisation, classification, or labelling of its items. The psycho-physical and the psycho-biochemical processes of human brain are beyond any imagination.

Human awareness may be divided broadly into two – 'Generic and Specific.' It is difficult to distinguish the awareness as either internal or external. It is like fluttering of the wings of a bee. As a bee moves from flower to flower, so does awareness move from one interest to another. Even when the bee settles on one flower and extracting the nectar, its wings are moving rapidly. Similarly, the sphere of consciousness is very rapid.

There are 16 aspects of the altering states of awareness: *Generic, Specific, Gross, Subtle, Causal, Turiyam, Senses, Mind, Intellect, Two Items of Interest (Physical and Somatic), and Five Vital Breaths (five Pranas: Prana, Apana, Samana, Vyana, and Udana.)* The real awareness constitutes the knowledge of these 16 aspects of the varied states of awareness. Where there is '*BHĀNA*' (basic awareness), there exists these aspects potentially.

The occasional bouts of physical and mental lassitude are common. Such states prevail only for short periods. Then the glow of life again resumes its brightness, and we can feel in our navel the urgency to prepare for a fresh venture. This awareness is of two types – generic and specific (external and internal).

The discovery of 'Self' is the discovery of Truth. Truth is stranger than fiction. It will turn our understanding of the world 180 degree from where it stands now. With the discovery of the Self, all that has been accumulated for centuries will turn out to be mere phantom details of information. The senses, mind, intellect, the objects of interests, and the five vital breaths are the instruments for learning the Self. The *tamas* (ignorance) can envelope the individuated consciousness in such a way that *satva* (idea) is cut off from opportunities. Such a state can be described as *sushupti* (deep sleep). This is similar to a sperm imprisoned in a seed waiting for an opportunity to come up. Opportunity is called *kaarana* and the reason behind *kararana* is *Bhāna* (awareness).

The fundamental truth of a pot is the clay. This truth is veiled by the transactional emphasis on the artefact of other things. Where there is awareness, there is consciousness and light. But unfortunately, as the eye does not see itself, so the Self by the Self. The discovery of the Self will turn our understanding one hundred and eighty degrees from where it stands now. Human beings are under the clutches of superimpositions and what is superimposed is unreal and what is not superimposed, that alone is real and Godly.

Management Concepts of *Bhāna Darśanam*

[VISION OF AWARENESS]

(The Ability to Perceive a Situation or Fact)

"It is the intense spirituality of India, and not any great political structure or social organisation that it has developed, which has enabled it to resist the ravages of time and the accidents of history..."

— **Dr. Sarvepalli Radhakrishnan**

"Bhāna Darśanam is Vision of Awareness", better say, "Vision of Self Awareness." The basic key for Self Awareness is spirituality.

When Steve Jobs was asked, by a friend, *"What he should do to become as successful as Steve?"*, the instant reply was *"go to India for spiritual knowledge."*

Arjuna was a worldly person struggling with his own issues; Krishna's message helped him overcome challenges and emerge victorious. Like *Bhagavad Gita,* the *Darśana Mālā* introduces us to our inner personality – the body, soul, mind, and intellect. Intellect is the controlling factor. It must be fortified to hold the urges of the body and put the whims and fancies of the mind in place. Many of our actions are performed automatically and unconsciously. It is a normal linear flow sans any motive. On the other hand, **"if one becomes aware of his actions, the results would be amazingly different. When the intellect is in command, you tap into your talent and achieve success."**

This *Darsana* is the 'Vision of Awareness'. A true businessman is a wisdom seeker and he distinguishes between "What Is" and "What Ought To Be". It helps him to know where he stands at present and in which direction he should move to further his goals. Here he comes across a cursory review of his immediate stand.

Every day and every moment of his wakeful life, the businessman bears a constant barrage of new stimuli and confronts with varied demands which warrant a thorough awareness of the situations which he deals with. This awareness is the un-slipping consciousness of 'first-rate-clarity.' The physical or mental lassitude or the lackadaisical or un-inspirational attitude is unwelcome here. Inspiration, fresh energy and impetus can easily initiate and sustain transactions in the work-a-day world of constant competition. It helps one to take the road less travelled. The knowledge of the Self is as wings to man's life, and a ladder for his ascent.

The counterpart of this is the world of dream where the operational efficiency of the manoeuvring consciousness is reduced to its minimum and awareness is very much of the nature of a passive witness to the phantasms of imagination. In this *Darsana,* Guru invites us and makes us familiar with the "Sixteen Aspects of the Altering States of Awareness." They are the awareness of "*Generic, Specific, Gross, Subtle, Causal, Turiam, Senses, Mind, Intellect, and Two Items of Interest (Physical, Somatic),* plus Five Vital Breaths *(Pranas)* – *Prana, Apana, Samana, Vyana, and Udana.* The gifted luminaries use these varied states of awareness to guide the destiny of the world.

As with the eye which cannot see itself, so the 'Self' does not see itself; the Self is not the object of consciousness, the Self sees the object of consciousness. Consciousness is of two kinds – the 'Generic' and the 'Specific'. The consciousness of "I" or "This" is Generic; whereas the consciousness of the "Absolute" is Specific. An individual, whether businessman or leader, must have the generic consciousness (otherwise called the Self-consciousness) to be a leading personality. The vision of consciousness is like a pendant that might hang in a necklace of gems strung together from the most central gem.

Hindu philosophy postulates that everything in this world is a part of the same entity; the creator and the created are really one and the same thing. Therefore there is no point in hating others as they are really a part of you. "Treating others equals; consider others as peers; participating others as fellow workers" is a very hot HR practice in business world. We are all made in God's image. We are all a reflection, a representation of the 'Infinite Creator'. We are all drops in the ocean of God. This is why it is so important to have compassion towards each other. When you harm others, you harm yourself.

In our daily life we are kept awake by a constant barrage of new stimuli. If we do not have a continuous encounter demanding our full awareness to deal with them, the consciousness slips into a second-or-third-rate condition of vanity. Everything is created by the mind – reasoning, fantasizing, and philosophising. The 'Grey Matter' of human brain conceals many secrets in it and the psychological and the psycho-bio-chemical phenomena created are fantastic of which no biochemist nor the psychologist has any deep idea. One must be a *Yogi* to learn such awareness which is beyond the reach of an average brain. Hence, Guru advocates meditation/yoga for entrepreneurs.

The 'created' and the 'creation' are one and the same; the cause and effect are not two but one; and hence, 'business man' and the business are not two entities, but one (unity), and when and only when such deep commitment comes, the business will be at its zenith of growth. The 'clayness' of clay cannot be taken away from it; the clay may appear in any fashion or artefact – a pot, a jug, a vase, or a plate. These are the differentia of clay, but the fundamental quality is not changed, it is 'clayness'. Similarly, a business is what the business man is.

'*BHĀNA*' means basic awareness, as said earlier. A business man of this basic consciousness would recognise what is what and who is who. He will be able to distinguish between 'clay' and 'pot'. Identifying pot is 'general consciousness'; whereas finding the 'clay' in the pot is his 'specific consciousness'. A leader shall have both the 'generic' as well as the 'specific' awareness. Guru suggests 'meditation' to sharpen this faculty of differentiation.

Guru says, to distinguish between the 'generic-specific' awareness, one should concentrate on to his "Senses, Mind, Intellect, the Items of Interest, and the Five Vital Breaths". The *'Bhāna Darsana'* is conceived in accordance with the frame of reference of the *'Mandukya Upanishad'*. The Upanishad is favoured by the 'Non-dualistic' school of Vedanta. It represents the 'Monistic' or 'Non-dual' philosophy. Sree Narayana Gurudev was the famous proponent of "Non-dual Philosophy". "Know the 'Self'" is its canon; knowing the 'Self' means knowing the 'Absolute'. And to know the 'Absolute' via knowing the 'Self', one should know *'Bhāna Darsana'*.

A Guru is sometimes described as *'sarvalokaanurupaya'* – one who can enter into complete empathy with all states of everyone, transcending all barriers of convention, tradition, and structural norms. A common man reaches this stage when he goes into deep sleep. In deep sleep, for him, there is no name or form, neither morality nor immorality, nor he ignorant or learned, and the entire matrix of values and relationships are in oblivion, and it is this freedom that is glorified as true bliss. A *'sarvalokaanurupaya'* leader is a Great HR Manager.

All sentient beings look for common good. When one's thoughts and activities are directed towards the attainment of the common collective good, that sentient being is free from social ego and attains the status of a man of unitive action, which makes him a *'karma yogi'*. Such a being sees the one Supreme God in every atom of the Universe and he feels in his very being the magnanimous benevolence of his Lord. Such a soul is free from ego, relativistic attachment or hatred, and no matter whether 'Actual' or 'Perceptual', feels only equality of beingness; equal minded towards all beings; a knower of true Absolute. So, where there is *'Bhāna'* (basic awareness) in management, operating as personal awareness, it is said to be 'Conscious Management'; where there is absent of *'Bhāna'*, it is said to be merely the prattling of an ignoramus, and certitude springs. It is the theory of Awareness of the Concrete. It is the hub on which the wheels of man's activities turn. In fine, *Bhāna Darśanam* is *"The Theory of Awareness" (or "The Theory of Conscious Management")*.

A manager must perceive and conceive, and must be in the wakeful consciousness. As a man thinks in his heart, so is he. He must 'Re-cognise' the sixteen aspects of the altering states of awareness and must succeed. Human body is a holistic system, enabling us to think, feel, and evaluate. *Bhāna Darsana* transforms the basic consciousness into the awareness of a concrete experience. Guru says that awareness is of, basically, four kinds – over and above the 'Generic' and the 'Specific' differentiation – Gross, Subtle, Causal, and Pure Consciousness or *turiyam*. In the absence of this awareness, *'tamas'* can envelop the individuated consciousness and *'satva'* is cut off and *'rajas'* absent and the personal 'Self' may slip into deep sleep and we can describe such a state as *'susupti'*. It is similar to a sperm (gene) imprisoned in a seed waiting for an opportunity to germinate. *Bhāna Darsana* focuses on the "RE-cognition" of these aspects of awareness which are confined in the depth of consciousness, and Guru describes this recognition as *KARANA (the Cause)* – the Cause for 'Self Development.'

"The Self is the one seer behind all that is seen, though it sees not itself; the one listener behind all hearing, though it hears not itself; the one knower behind all knowing, though it knows not itself; and the one enjoyer behind all enjoyment, though it enjoys not itself."(1) When there is 'Awareness of Self', then the cryptic

formula does manifest before us – '*That Alone Exists*' (*tadeva sat*). It is the 'Awareness Paramount;' it is the Awareness of the Absolute; it is the Awareness of the Self. When a Leader achieves this knowledge, then he starts to 'Takes Off' into the vast infinite Blue Sky. He and his business are now in 'Take Off' stage of growth with all the advanced technology, sufficient resources and Management marvels, as depicted by W.W. Rostow. *It is the precious pendant and the secret key of the entire "Garland of Visions."*

[Recapitulation: (DISCOVERY OF THE SELF) A Manager/ Leader must be Awaresome and Conscious. The development of the 'Self' is the mother of all developments]

Bhāna Darśanam

1. Nitya Chaitanya Yati, (1987), "*The Psychology of Darśana Mālā,*" Gurukulam Publishing House, Fernhill – Varkala – Bainbridge, p.280.

Chapter 6

KARMA DARŚANAM

Meaning:

Man acts and reacts, or so he universally thinks and therefore it is only natural that man understands all perceived changes in terms of actions and reactions, causes and consequences. The duality of the world of 'cause and effect' shall be together when we act: the sun has no motivation, and it simply radiates its effulgence; the formation of the planets, and their motions; the earth being habitable; the solar energy and moisture getting into various kinds of alchemy to produce life of all sorts of this planet, are all its evidences. The 'Self' alone, through MĀYĀ, does action by assuming many forms... I think, I speak, I grasp. I hear... all such forms of action are done by only the 'Supreme Self'. The 'I-consciousness' is functioning fully aided by the senses and the mind. The Self has some kind of power, inseparable from it, difficult to define, and by that alone all actions are projected. The one Self alone burns as fire, blows as wind, showers as rain, supports as earth, and flows as river.

The six aspects – existence, birth, growth, change, deterioration, and extinction – happen here. Everything in the Universe – from mighty stars in the galaxy to tiny atoms – is subject to change, decay and diffusion. Thus the worlds of macrocosm and microcosm, and of subjective phenomena are all belonging to the same order of change and transformation. Mere repression of action will produce only inner conflict, and as a consequence more action of the worst kind come up. The 'Self' is the basis of all apparent actions. Knowledge or wisdom lies in knowing the secrets of the impetus of action and the phantom-like manifestations of the phenomenal cosmos happen.

By means of the inner organ and the senses, action becomes self-accomplished. A wise man, therefore, can always look upon himself as having no programme of action. He knows "I am the unattached, inner well-founded one." A wise man realises the worthlessness and knows that his senses, physical organism, and mind are all integral parts of the phenomenal universe. No matter what the action or what demands is made on him, he will maintain the sameness of vision. He will keep himself always in a state of neutral zero, i.e., *sthithaprajna*.

Every action of a wise man will arise from and contain within itself a mystical quality of love, kindness, compassion, or beauty. He is in harmony with the universal Self, and sees everywhere nothing but truth. This truth is the light which illuminates the oneness of all things. What he continually sees and understands as truth are the unalloyed expressions of goodness and beauty, and hence he experiences happiness. One who is wise does not limit such happiness to the egoistic appreciation of an object of pleasure or pain. The actions of one who is wise are unitive and resonate with wisdom.

Management Concepts of *Karma Darśanam*

[VISION OF ACTION]

(The Ability to Recognise the Significance of Action)

> "The philosophy of action is that no one else is the giver of peace or happiness. One's own karma, one's own actions are responsible to being either happiness or success or whatever."

> **– Maharishi Mahesh Yogi**

Karma Darśanam is Vision of Action. It is also known as 'Vision of Cosmo-Psychological Functionalism.'

'Karma' is the spiritual equivalent to Newton's *Third Law of Motion* (*Law of Action-Reaction*) in Physics, which reads: *"For every action there is an equal and opposite reaction."*[1] 'Whatever action we do, it incurs a reaction' is the message of the infallible Law of Action and Reaction. If we put out positive loving energy, we receive positive loving energy in return. If we put out negative energy in the form of judgemental attitudes or dishonesty, that same type of energy comes back to us. This is the 'Law of *Karma*.' This has reference to "Change Management".[2]

If the mirror is coloured, the reflection will also be coloured. If the mirror has a concave surface, the image looks enlarged. If it is convex, the image looks shrunken. See the Biblical narration: *"Judge not, that ye be not judged. For with what judgement ye judge, ye shall be judged: and with what measure ye mete, it shall be measured to you again."*[3]

The *Bhagavad Gita* recites:

"Karmanye Vadhitkaraste-
Ma Phaleshu Kada Chana,
Ma Karma Phala Hetur
Bhurmatey Sangostva Akarmani."[4]

[*You have the right to perform your prescribed duty, but you are not entitled to the fruits of action. Never consider yourself to be the cause of the results of your activities, and never be attached to not doing your duty.*]

The cognitive, conative, and affective consciousness functions and engages in actions continously. The Sun has no motivation. It simply radiates its light and heat. So many things are caused by the sheer presence of the Sun – the formation of the planets, their motions, the earth becoming habitable and the solar energy and moister getting into various kinds of alchemy to produce life of all sorts on this planet.

The Guru wants to show us that individual action is part and parcel of Cosmic Action; and the cosmic action is 'action-less' action, having no actor behind it. Man is not a stranger in, or a visitor to, this universe; he is an integral part of it. Hence, his action and reaction are very important. As integral part of the cosmos, we are also governed by the laws of nature. Where action ceases altogether is described as *NIRVĀNA*. A person who spends time indulging in pleasure and luxury rather than dealing with practical concerns is what is called a **'Lotus Eater.'** 'He is not only un-productive, but is also a looter, and his taking of food and drinks may akin to a theft', in terms of Gandhiji. He upsets the **'Apple Cart'** of common economy and ruins the productivity and spoils someone's plans.

The Sun rises in the east, becomes warm and bright in the mid-day, giving energy to all and sundry, then sets in the west. Night falls with its gentle and soothing moon-shine and star-light. Clouds which rise from the bosom of the ocean to float in the sky and to discharge rain on the farmers' crops. The physical universe is so constituted that physical and chemical properties are produced without the intervention of any personal will. The sun shines, the wind blows, the cloud rains, the river flows... all are due to a Universal will. The fine network of the nervous system, the conveyance of nerve impulses, the secretions from our glands,...... and the metabolic changes in our body... all operate with perfect inner co-ordination. *'Nishkama Karma'* is the philosophy of Nature. Guru gives the incidence of action of fire, of wind, of clouds, of rivers, and of the concrete inner cohesion of the Earth as examples of occurrences in the cosmic Self. These are governed by the precise laws of Nature. We, unconsciously, attribute personification to Natural Events. We are an integral part of the Universe, so that, we are also governed by the Laws of

Nature. Thus, *Karma Darśanam* is aptly named *as "The Theory of Nishkāma Karma" (or "The Theory of Undesirous Action ").*

Every action of a wise man will arise from and contain within itself an altruistic or mystical quality of love, kindness, compassion, or beauty. Such a man is in harmony with the Universal Self. In the corporate world, one leader must attempt to relate the individual Self with the corporate Self. He sees nothing but truth everywhere. This truth is the light which illuminates the oneness of all things.

Gurujian take is that "what is good for long-term is *'shrēyas'*; what is good for short term is". Guru's *'shrēyas-prēyas'* dichotomy is reflected in the *Vishāda Yoga* in Mahābhārata. Arjuna refuses to engage in battle (in the *Mahābhārata* war) as he analyses the three concepts of life – bodily conception, mental conception, and intellectual conception – and asks Krishna, "I am bewildered about my duty; tell me what is good for me in *'shrēyas.'* Arjuna seeks a long-term view and so too should a leader. Krishna answers:[5]

"Seek refuge in divine knowledge and insight, O Arjun, and discard reward-seeking actions that are certainly inferior to works performed with the intellect established in Divine knowledge."

"The one who prudently practices the science of work without attachment can get rid of both good and bad reactions in this life itself."

"The wise endowed with equanimity of intellect, abandon attachment to the fruits of actions, which bind one to the cycle of life and death. By working in such consciousness, they attain the state beyond all sufferings."

"When your intellect crosses the quagmire of delusion, you will then acquire indifference to what has been heard and what is yet to be heard."

An Entrepreneur-Leader must render *Nishkama Karma* to grow; he must be a *Sthithaprajna* to advance. He needs to have both for the well-being of people at his command; needs to strike a balance between *prēyas* and *shrēyas* – short-term in the context of 'body-mind-intellect' well-being and long-term in the context of 'spiritual' well-being.

The Chetwode Motto[6] reads: *"The safety, honour and welfare of your country come first, always and every time. The honour, welfare and comfort of the men you command come next. Your own ease, comfort and safety come last, always and every time."* This shall be the proud credo of a corporate leader. The Guru's total life – childhood, youth, penance, old age – walk, talk, and his very being on the Earth were dedicated to the honour of the country and for the welfare of fellow human beings. The Guru was different from other *sanyasis* in the sense that he preferred to work in the society amongst his people so as to flow his enlightenment upon them for uplifting them.

Ravana, Hiranyakasipu, Kamsa, Duryodhana...were all able kings but only as far as 'body-mind-intellect' well-being is concerned. The 'spiritual' well-being aspect was absent in their cases. Krishna reveals to Arjuna that the war was more than a family feud; Krishna wanted Yudhishtira to rule Hastinapur, not Duryodhana, for he would take care of the fourth aspect – the 'spiritual well-being' (the 'spiritual aspect') of the people, too, in the kingdom. It is the duty of a good leader. As spiritual well-being is reckoned with, there shall no longer be greed, awry, and society will progress to a higher quality of life, resulting in holistic development and progress.

The actions of one who is wise are unitive and resonate with wisdom. Though engaged in the most complex of actions, his inner serenity will not be disturbed. No matter what the action or what demands is made on him, he will maintain the sameness of vision which is characteristic of a *yogi*.

There shall be *Karuna* (compassion) *in karma*... the sympathetic pity and concern for the sufferings or misfortunes of others. All living beings are parts or extensions of one's own Self. Buddhism upholds that there is no "other"; Hinduism says: "I am *Brahma*, so are you!". All beings are manifestations of *Brahma*, there is an essential identity among all beings. So, separation or alienation from others amount to alienation from oneself. Do no harm to others through your action. The one who acts out of compassion does not do so for his personal benefit. He does not act even for the psychological satisfaction of being instrumental in alleviating the others sufferings. Any true action of compassion does not even originate from the feeling: "I would like to see him not suffering; I do not come to it at all". It is a spontaneous act done for its own sake, not for self-satisfaction. Then it becomes *'Nishkama karma'*. It is *'actus purus'*, means 'pure action.'

Interaction with surroundings *(Nishkama Karma)* relaxes the mind, heart, and body. *Nishkama Karma* – action without desire for fruits – is refraining from not doing prescribed action, and then the equipoise in success, failure, and pain would lead to a state of equanimity.

The action should be *dharmic* and is to be done with a total sense of devotion and dedication. Gita says that one has choice only regarding action, not regarding the results thereof. Karma yoga emphasises to perform action with the attitude that results are shaped by the 'Laws of Nature' and the results come from Divine. Guru Vidura advices Pandavas in Mahābhārata, *"Do unto others what you wish to be done to you."*

Bill Gates, having renounced his position in Microsoft Corporation, now dedicates his energy in the service of the society.

After having had his fill of power and position as the President of the USA, Bill Clinton now preaches the glories of service to humankind, and had even written a book entitled, *"Giving – How Each Of Us Can Change The World."* Let it be the aim of a new-gen leader. May it be the *karmic marg* (pursuit of action) of a modern Business Leader?

[Recapitulation: (UNDESIROUS ACTION) The businessman must be an Activist with Enthusiastic fervour. The Dedicated Action is his motto]

Karma Darśanam

1. Sir Isaac Newton, (1687), *"Philosophiae Naturalis Principia Mathematica"* (Mathematical Principles of Natural Philosophy), Third Law of Motion (Law of Action-Reaction).

2. Kotter, John P., the *Konosuke Matsushita* Professor of Leadership, Emeritus at the Harvard Business School, the USA.

3. *The Bible*, Matthew 7:1, King James version.

4. *Bhagavad Gita*, Chapter II, verse 47.

5. ibid, verses 49–52.

6. Field Marshal Philip Walhouse Chetwode, British Army (1869 – 1950), at the Inauguration of the Indian Military Academy on 10 December 1932, he expressed this motto.

Chapter 7

JÑĀNA DARŚANAM

Meaning:

Jñāna Darśanam is the holistic vision of the total awareness of the Self. There is a broad division of awareness of the Self – the 'Unconditioned Awareness of the Self', and the 'Conditioned Awareness of the Self.' They are known as *'Nirupadhikam'* and *'Sopadhikam'* *(Nirupadhika Jñānam and Sopadhika Jñānam)* respectively. To illustrate this general division, the two terms – *'idanta'* and *'ahanta'* – can be used. *'Idanta'* means pertaining to 'thisness' and *'ahanta'*, means pertaining to the 'Self' or 'I Consciousness.'

Jñāna Darsana is to release the mind from all painful conditioning and to lead it to its original state of pure 'Unconditional Consciousness.' The Self can be compared to a light that can see and is always witnessing whatever it illuminates. When things are known as they are, as in the knowledge of the truth of rope, then it is factual knowledge, and the knowledge will be fictitious when it is otherwise. To see rope as rope is right knowledge and to see the rope as snake is a wrong knowledge.

The pure knowledge is none other than the Self-knowledge. The nature of the Self is pure existence (*sat*), pure awareness (*cit*), and the supreme value (*ananda*). The three constituents of nature are *satva, rajas*, and *tamas*. Realization comes only when all three of these modalities of nature are transcended. It is a broad division of the awareness of the Self and it is none other than the 'Pure Awareness of the Self'. It is the Pure Consciousness, without becoming a participant in the "I" and "mine" roles of the ego. Such a state is termed *SAT-CHIT-ĀNANDA, i.e.,* "existence" *(SAT)* in "pure awareness" *(CHIT),* and "keeping the supreme value" *(ĀNANDA).* This means that within ourselves we have a normative notion of value.

The real or absolute knowledge is the beingness of knowledge.

Management Concepts of *Jñāna Darśanam*

[VISION OF CONSCIOUSNESS]

(The Ability to Understand and Act)

> *"The world is full of obvious things which nobody by any chance ever observes."*

> — **Arthur Conan Doyle**

It is the 'Vision of Awareness' (Knowledge). It can also be called Vision of Consciousness and its Modifications. It introduces the holistic vision of total awareness of the Self. The awareness of the Self is divided in to the "Unconditioned" and the "Conditioned" (*nirupadhikam* and *sopadhikam*).

In a more precise definition, it is *atma Jñāna* (knowledge of Sel-realisation). It is "Vision by Knowledge" and it introduces us to the holistic vision of the total awareness of the Self. Here, Guru advises "Self Management." So, the sum and substance of *Jñāna Darśanam* is **Self Management."**

Sree Narayana Guru makes a distinction between *atma Jñāna* (knowledge of the Self) and *Vastu ViJñāna* (knowledge of things). Guru calls our attention to the traditional example, that of the correct perception of rope as rope and the erroneous perception of rope as snake. He says that to perceive rope as a rope is actual knowledge, but to see rope as snake is illusionary knowledge.

"In a good library we shall see a large stock of impressive looking books, the authors of which lay claim to the revelation of truth. How many billions of trees have been reduced to pulp to provide the paper for the endless output of books and how many man-hours have gone into their production is unknown."[1] It is likely that one who does seek the Self will eventually turn away from such treasures of recorded wisdom to the unrecorded truth of his own beingness.

The more you know, the more you don't know. Scientists say that the observable Universe is about 46 billion light years in radius. And they accept that there is an un-observable Universe that they are not able to fathom yet. Whenever man becomes proud that he has made a fantastic discovery, then the Universe tells, "Sorry, you have a long way to go." It means that, eventually, what man does is always a work-in-progress, not a finished product.

The vision of awareness aims at a "Creative Mind". In simple sense, it is Awareness without Ego. "Knowing things as they really are" is the real awareness; otherwise rope shall be mistaken as snake. This awareness is the empirical awareness, and it is also called the transcendental awareness. It is a way of a positive thinking and there is no difference between subject and object. If you do something, as a matter of conscious planning, it will make your mind creative. But, if you do something as a habit, then it will not develop creative thinking. Doing something as a result of conscious planning develops a person's mind and leads to creative thinking. All the successful business luminaries have proven their creative minds. Here, they use both the hemispheres of their brain effectively – the left hemisphere for **Cognitive Skills** and the right hemisphere for the

'Transcendental Skills,' – and especially giving weightage to the right-half. Here, there is the summation of *Yin* and *Yang* philosophies in a balance. So, *Jñāna Darśanam* may be pretty confidently qualified as *"The Theory of Transcendental Awareness," (or "The Theory of Self Management")*.

Guru Sree Narayana is a monist philosopher and a thought leader, giving particularised (personalised) interests to both physio-spiritual aspects on equal terms. It is called "Integral Philosophy", which treats both 'matter' and 'spirit' as semantic variations. This knowledge is named *'paraJñāna'*, means 'Transcendental Knowledge'. It is a free and universal consciousness by itself and for itself. What is diametrically opposite to it is the knowledge which is 'specific and focussed' of sense interest, called *'IndriyaJñāna'* which means 'sensory knowledge'. These two are the extreme limits of knowledge – *apogee and perigee* – and all other modifications come in between these two extremes like a spectrum interwoven with intelligence and sensations, as follows:

> *ParaJñāna* (transcendental knowledge)
>
> *JivaJñāna* (individuating knowledge)
>
> *SopadhikaJñāna* (relativistic knowledge)
>
> *NirupadhikaJñāna* (unconditional knowledge)
>
> *PratyaksaJñāna* (direct perception)
>
> *YatharthaJñāna* (valid knowledge)
>
> *AyatharthaJñāna* (invalid knowledge)
>
> *ParoksaJñāna* (perceived by another)
>
> *AparoksaJñāna* (inwardly perceived knowledge)
>
> *AnumitiJñāna* (Inferential knowledge)
>
> *UpamitiJñāna* (comparative knowledge)
>
> *AtmaJñāna* (knowledge of self-realisation)
>
> *AnatmaJñāna* (knowledge of the non-self)
>
> *IndriyaJñāna* (sensory knowledge).

As said earlier, *Jñāna Darśanam* is the holistic vision of the total awareness of the 'Self.' The term 'Self' has only one connotation: "*sat-cit-ānanda*" (existence-knowledge-bliss). To be more precise, Self is pure existence (*sat*), pure awareness (*cit*), and the supreme value (ĀNANDA). The 'Self' has 'Absolute Existence' and 'Self' is to be seen as 'Absolute Existence.' The 'Self' is the source of all awareness. It is the real wealth, the greatest weapon, asset, strength, and power. The pure awareness animates all individuated beings as well as animating the cosmos. **Self Management** is to still the chattering mind. Krishna tells Arjuna: "*the bliss supreme accrues to the person whose mind has been stilled, who is egoless, and who is convinced that God alone is.*"[2] Stilling the chattering mind seems to be the key to attain peace and peace leads to success and the success leads to bliss.

A fragment of knowledge is dangerous; a total awareness is often vivified. The total awareness arrive at "*aum, tat, sat*", meaning "that alone Is". The *mahāvākya*, "*tat tvamasi*", meaning, "that thou art" a still vivid perception of "*aum tat sat*". This *aum* alone is the pith and core of *Jñāna Darśanam*. It is the unconditioned knowledge. The unconditioned knowledge is indescribable, so that, rishis use the sound "*aum*" to indicate it. The monosyllable '*aum*' is the Absolute. The indivisible and all-embracing knowledge is '*aum*'; it is indicated as the Absolute. The Absolute is everything. So, '*aum tat sat*' are employed differently to describe the indescribable, all three terms have become so semantically rich as to each stand singularly for the Absolute: '*aum*'means the Absolute; '*tat*' means the Absolute; '*sat*'means the Absolute. "*Aham Brahmāsmi, tat tvamasi*", means "I am the Absolute, and so you are." In fine, everything is Brahma or the manifestation of the Absolute and the Absolute is the Universal Knowledge. So, when you know yourself (know your 'Self'), then you know the God, and it is the greatest knowledge. It is the stage of enlightenment.

A ruler or a leader must be a '*Rājarshi*' (*Rāja* + *Rishi*): he must have the power of a king to act and the enlightenment of an *Rishi* to think before act. "He is large, he contains multitudes," (indebted to the brainy quote, "...I am large, I contain multitudes", of Walt Whitman,[3] the American poet). He celebrates the theme of democracy and the oneness. As well, it represents Transcendentalist thought.

Guru had installed a 'Mirror' in one of his temples (temple at Kadakamkonam) for devotees as the 'Idol' for worship. The devotee sees his image on the mirror and he sees the image which is created by himself. The image is the testimony of one's existence created by himself and the image is not actually himself, but still he believes that it is 'he' – it is a 'virtual he'. Who is the real 'he'? The observer, the observed, and the observation are critical and interconnected deeply and what the image appears on the mirror is the objective perception of his consciousness. To know one's real 'Self', he needs Self-awareness. 'Self-awareness' is using mirror neurons for 'looking at oneself' for conscious recognition of Self. Until one sees himself on the mirror, he maintains a 'Superposition'. This 'Superposition' is an adulterated 'me', full of a confused state by conditioning, biases, and complexes of limitations. Unless and until one leader recognises his superposition and comes down to his real Self, the business being led by him remains a cage of sparrow at the tip of the tree-branch, oscillating in the unruly wind.

The first principle of 'Self Management' is to understand the Self; the second principle is to hold a mirror to oneself; the third one is not to understand oneself on the basis of other people's opinions and views; the fourth is developing one's competence and to learn one's strengths and weaknesses; the fifth principle is to concentrate mind on only one thing at a time; the sixth is to sharpen memory; the seventh is Self constraint; and finally the eighth is good communication skills. All these Self Management Principles can be improved with meditation (*preksha dhyana*). Here, 'seeing' does not mean external vision, but careful concentration on subtle consciousness by mental insight. "See You Thyself" is the fundamental theme of *Preksha Dhyana*.[4] Its aim is purification of emotions, psyche, consciousness, and the realization of the Self.

Jñāna Yoga of Ramana Maharshi pursues the question: '*Who am I?*'; *Karma Yoga* of Gandhiji asks: '*Who preferred work without attachment?*'; and *Bhakti Yoga* of saint Tukaram inquires: '*Who surrendered his mind totally to the Supreme?*' All these *yajnas* toil to explain the hard core principle of 'Self Management' propounded by Sree Narayana Guru in *Jñāna Darśanam* of *Darśana Mālā*.

In fine, the 'Self Management' is the real science of Business Management. The successful business Magnates, knowingly or un-knowingly, follow the canons of Self Management. Passing through various strides, such a transcendental leader will guide his Organisation to head for '**Pre Drive to Maturity**' stage of growth now.

[Recapitulation: (TRANSCENDENTAL AWARENESS) The Businessman must be Self-Managed. He must be a *Rajarshi*, (Raja + Irshi); a person of thorough Consciousness and its modifications]

Jñāna Darśanam

1. Nitya Chaitanya Yati, (1987), "*The Psychology of Darśana Mālā,*" Gurukulam Publishing House, Fernhill – Varkala _ Bainbridge, p.342.

2. *Bhagavad Gita*, 6:17.

3. Whitman, Walt., (1855), *"Song of Myself,"* Dover Publications, America, 51:3.8 Reprint, Shambhala (1998), ISBN 1570623694, 9781570623691.

4. https://www.speekingtree.in>preksha meditation.

Chapter 8

BHAKTI DARŚANAM

Meaning:

Meditation on the Self is '*Bhakti.*' The knower of the Self always meditates. Sequentially, meditation comes as a prelude to contemplation. Meditation on the Self is *bhakti,* by which the self is blissful, with that the knower of the 'Self' always meditates up on the 'Self' by the 'Self'. It is the 'total imploration' of the depth of whatever is to be known. The way to know something is not by going around it, but by first entering into it and then being it. 'The state of actually being it is' is what is achieved by contemplation. It is the continuous meditation on one's own true nature.

The constant meditation on Brahma – the Absolute – is *Bhakti.* It is also called *Dhyana* in Sanskrit. *Dhyana* means the 'pure state of contemplation.' *Atma, Brahma,* and Ānanda fall into the vertical line of *Bhakti.* It is the trio of '*sat – chit – ānanda.*' The wise man sees joy everywhere, since his *bhakti* is the highest. I am Ānanda, I am *Brahma*, I am *atma* and he knows '*aham brahma aasmi.*' Pure action (*actus purus*) emanates from him. Love, devotion, empathy, and consequent rapture of mind come spontaneously from him.

Adi Sankara, in his '*Vivekachudamani*' (the crest jewel of wisdom discrimination) defined '*bhakti*' as "*svasvarupaanusandhanum bhaktith.*", meaning "contemplation (*bhakti*) is the continuous meditation (*anusandhanaum)* on one's own true nature (*svasvarupa*)". Narada's *Bhakti Sutra* holds '*bhakti*' as "Absolute Love", which can also mean "Love for the Absolute." The non-duality is the essence of *bhakti* and original non-duality is the absolution. Self-knowledge recognises (recognises) the singular homogeneity in subject and object, knower and known, actor and action, or the enjoyer and the enjoyed. Where such a union is realised, the knower of the self is absolved of all prejudicial judgements that prevent the natural flow of love. Buddha, Lao-tzu, Christ and other perfected beings are well known for their compassion and unlimited liability to the entire world. This is *bhakti*.

It is vision by love. In *Narada's Bhakti Sutra, bhakti* is 'absolute love', which can also mean 'love for the Absolute'. The reciprocation of giving and receiving love between the lover and the beloved characterises the ever-abiding need for togetherness and the un-diminishing appreciation of each other. All beings are always, by their own nature, driven to seek such union.

Constant meditation on *Brahma* is thus known as *Bhakti*. Love is shown as a unifying dynamic. The same love, in its perfection of actualisation, is an ever-abiding rejoicing in the highest sense of mystical union with all. Absolute is exemplified in the lives of Buddha, Lao-tzu, Jesus Christ, and other perfect beings who are all known for their compassion and unlimited *bhakti* (love).

Management Concepts of *Bhakti Darśanam*

[VISION OF CONTEMPALTION]

(The Ability to think profoundly with love)

> *"To love is to be in communion with the other and to discover in that other the spark of God."*

> **– Paulo Coelho**

Bhakti Darśanam is 'Vision of Contemplation.' It is the 'Vision of Contemplative Devotion.' It is the ability to think profoundly. It is contemplative devotion and the term *Bhakti* is defined as *the continuous contemplation of one's Self."* A continuous contemplation on anything leads to normalcy and love. Hence *Bhakti Darśanam* is also named 'Vision of Love."

[Synonyms for contemplation are thought, meditation, consideration, pondering, reflection, thinking, nursing, rumination, deliberation, cogitation, reverie, concentration, and introspection and so on and so forth.]

In his translation and commentary on *Darśana Mālā,* Nataraja Guru, calls *Bhakti Darsana as* "The Vision of Contemplation." Meditation and contemplation are often used as synonyms. Meditation is the prelude to contemplation. Contemplation means 'going into something' and then 'being it'. Meditation is the active 'imploration'.

Guru says, the knower of the 'Self' is always in a state of meditation. Guru's Vision by Contemplation stands not for milestone-hungry-management; rather it focuses on actions matching the needs of the society/organisation. Love reigns supreme where the fetters of the individual are broken; frontiers of visions are smashed; the perilous separation is averted; the ever deceiving symbols of 'you', 'he', 'she', 'it', 'that', 'this', and 'they' find no place. There is only 'One' always.' That One' is without a Second. It is the Brahma, the Absolute. One who contemplates reach to such a plain where he finds no 'Second.' And he recognises that ***Aham Brahma Asmi, Tat Tvam Asi*** [I am Brahma (the Absolute), Thou Art That].[1] It shows the Unity of macrocosm and microcosm. This *mahavakya* shall be the *mahamantra* of leaders of Business, Institutions, Organisations and that of Nations, so that, humanity will be respected, cosmic relationships will be protected, and cosmopolitan brotherhood will be flourished.

Geniuses like Vyasa, Valmiki, Homer, Dante, Shakespeare, Goethe,...or the creative abilities like Ravana, Arjuna, Karna, Romeo or an Othello... a ruler like Lincoln, Churchill, Gandhiji or others... the Buddha's *Nirvānā*, the Christ's *Thyaga,* or the Prophet's Love... all are one without a second. We need to de-toxify our mind, liberate it of all evil thoughts and intentions. Make sure that you do not even think about doing any harm to others. Negative thoughts cause harm to you. Use our imagination to think of alternatives to such negative thoughts, and it is contemplation. 'I', 'me', or 'mine' should go; Ego must go. Ego is 'Edging God Out' and hence it must go. The knower of the Self is said to be ever in contemplation of the Absolute. The Self-revealing consciousness is the *atma.* One who knows Self knows *atma,* and in turn it means that he knows *Brahma,* the Absolute. This pure state is *bhakti.* It is the awakening, liberation, emancipation, salvation, and self-realisation. And in its homogenous and unlimited vastness, there is no room for narrow thoughts of I-consciousness and for the symbols of 'you', 'he', 'she', 'it', 'they', 'this', and 'that'. Then there emerges love. Hence, *Bhakti Darśanam* is 'Vision of Love.'

The Wiseman sees everywhere nothing but joy of the Self – in the world regulated by physicochemical, biophysical, and biochemical laws – a subversion of the order of the trio of *SAT CHIT ĀNANDA.* He sees the triple manifestations of the illusory, the transactional, and the transcendental realms of business world. It is this efficiency that makes his contemplation the highest of all achievements. *Towards the father of the world, to one's spiritual teacher, father, or mother, towards the founders of truth, towards those who put down evil, towards those who do good to all, the wise man will act and pro-act indiscriminately the good, with indeterminable courage like little sparrows, however small in size and meagre in strength to defend, will valiantly put up all their might and courage to fight an intruding snake or crow that wants to gobble up their fledglings.*[2]

The energy that is used to resist, to reject, to defend, to offend, and to flee is killer energy and we must seek redress. The energy that is used to assist, to accept, to obey, to offer, and to combine is creative energy and we must sustain it. It is the desire of the Self. The wise man sees everywhere, nothing but, the joy of the Self. His *bhakti*, indeed, is the highest; his *bhakti* is true love. Mind is like the confluence of two streams, one bringing in the perceived data of an objective world regulated by physiochemical, biological, and biochemical laws, and the other constituted of imaginations, memories, and volitions geared by desires. The wise man goes for lent and silent contemplation and selects the true path of *bhakti* and love. That love is '*agape'*, means true love of the Absolute.

The *Bhakti Darsana* is summarily called "Vision of Love." What characterises a loving management is the ever-abiding need for togetherness and the un-diminishing appreciation between the management and the employees, as in the case of a couple reciprocating of giving and taking love between the lover and the beloved. It is an ever-abiding, rejoicing, all-embracing kindness as is exemplified in the life of Budhha, Lao-tzu, Jesus Christ, and other preferred beings. *Atma, Brahma*, and *Ānanda* fall in to the line of *bhakti*, and harmony and 'be-ness' prevail there.

Anything conditional, eventual, or consequential is not *bhakti* (love) and only the self-less and appreciation is *bhakti*. So, the relationship between the employer and the employees must be 'absolute, and unconditional.' Ignorance is an ocean of darkness, knowledge is the Island of light where rises the resplendent Sun of pure consciousness. Darkness is negative, and it conceals truth and obstructs vision, and it shades Vision of Love.

The I-consciousness in the mind of the employer or among other employees will be a hydra-headed myth. Deciphering this myth is awakening, liberation, emancipation, knowing the Tao, God-realisation, salvation, and self-realisation. Transparency, homogeneity, and 'one-ness' in the place of you, me, he, she, they, this, and that, prevail where the love reigns supreme. Vyasa, Valmiki, Homer, Dante, Shakespeare, Goethe, and others spread this love.

A true leader excels in maintaining his position in the neutral zero in tackling things. The 'Universal urge to care' is his dictum. As little sparrows' case mentioned earlier, however small in size and meagre in strength to defend, he will valiantly put up his might and courage to fight an intruding enemy or outside force, he will protect his people in high and lows. The entire corporate life can be described as an aggregate of values and a net work of relationships connecting and co-ordinating each other. A spontaneous involvement with oneself and each other among the whole and creates joy in the organisational ambience is an *actus purus* (pure action/pure actuality). It is in the pure joy that one experiences one's natural alignment with the incorporate. This imperiential selfsameness with general values and ethics would generate the contemplation of the Self and an affinity with the Absolute. It equates to the **"Nudge Theory"** of the American Economist and Nobel Laureate, Richard H. Thaler. By love, care and persuasion we can get things done by others. Coercion, manipulation, pull, pressure, dissuasion and the like are negative promotions which boomerang and hence un-advisable.

"Snehamaan-akhila-saaram-oozhiyil...(love is the cord which binds buds together in the cosmos...) is the Guru's philosophy and the true love *(bhakti)* is an intelligent key to unravel the science

of values and inter-relationships. It is the key to open the vault of Self-realisation. It is the pivot of human behavioural science. It is the sum-and-substance of inter-relationships in the incorporate entity. *Bhakti*, in essence, is the continuous contemplation of one's Self, whoever he/she is. It is the 'Vision of Love'/'Vision of Contemplation.' Meditation or contemplation is an active process of applying one's mind to make a 'Total Imploration' of the depth of whatever is to be known. It is the overwhelming recognition of 'be-ness' and 'loyalty.' It is the inevitable tool in the kitty of a successful entrepreneur. Hence, *Bhakti Darśanam* can be coined as *"The Theory of Love, Devotion, Compassion, and Empathy" (or "The Theory of Loyalty").*

It is the spectacular theory known for keeping relationship and productivity up. *"At the touch of love everyone becomes a poet,"* as Plato said. Lord Byron has aptly quoted that *"There is no instinct like that of the heart."* The Contemplation and love breed Devotion, Compassion, and Empathy in a corporate edifice. It soothes the hearts and emanates sense of belongingness among the corporate people and it ensures *esprit de corps* on office and work floors. 'Participative Management' and Considering Leadership will change the game incredibly. Rejig goal setting by love to tackle biz disruptions is a strategic management tip. Now the business, in the simile of Aeronautical metaphor, has reached the sufficient altitude. The highly significant fourth stage, **"Drive to Maturity,"** has been done successfully and henceforth the aircraft (business) will be in a level-fly, heading for the last 'Auto-piloting' stage at its growth path up in the infinite Blue Sky.

[Recapitulation: (LOVABLE, CONSIDERATE, AND EMPATHETICAL) Love is Game Changer. The Businessman must be Considerate, Lovable, and Empathetical to Co-ordinate and lead. Hire and fire is passé]

Bhakti Darśanam

1. *Chandogya Upanishad* 6.8.7, in the dialogue between Uddalaka and his son Svetaketu.

2. Nitya Chaitanaya Yati (1987), *"The Psychology of Darśanamala,"* Gurukula Publishing House, Fernhill-Varkala-Bainbridge, p.392.

Chapter 9

YOGA DARŚANAM

Meaning:

Those which always unite and also get united with *cidatma*, which is in the form of restraining mind, that is praised as *yoga*. Yoga is union – union of mind, soul, body, and spirit. The root cause of dis-unity lies in intrapersonal discords. Yoga is the beautiful incidence in which the knowledge of togetherness – of being one and identical – is beautifully complemented by the preparedness, to live in amity. In all the five senses of operations – locomotion, manipulation, articulation, procreation, and elimination – the human kind must seek the yoga and amity.

Yoga is union and it suggests the joining of things together. Disharmony causes disunity. The root cause of interpersonal disunity is the interpersonal heterogeneity. The great alchemy that can inter-relate two hearts through a process of fusing their interests in identical values comes from 'love.' The perceiver, the perceived, and the act of perception – all are visualised entirely by heart. The Yoga emanates from the heart. Thus the heart which is said to be the seat of ego also becomes the seat of intellect and love. Yoga is said to be love, the knowledge of togetherness. In yoga, there is no duality. That always unite and get united is yoga. The specific variance *'anya'* and the integrated universal *'sama'* stand equal. When this is achieved, one cuts across all forms of phenomena and gains the transparency of yogic vision. Then one realises that "All this is *Brahma*" ("*sarvam Khalvidam Brahma*").

Only the narrow minded discriminates "this one is mine and the other is a stranger." For those who live completive, the entire world constitutes but one family.

The root cause of interpersonal disunity lies in interpersonal discord. A great alchemy that can inter-relate two persons through a process of fusing their interests in identical values comes from the conflagration of love in which two such individuals are gracefully brought together by the Divine or by Benevolent Chance. Love is universally experienced as a process in which an effort of union is made through conscious aspiration and an effortless union is happening by Providential Grace. Yoga is such a link by which the knowledge of togetherness and oneness – of being one and identical – is complemented by the preparedness to live in amity.

Yoga is an incidence, better say a catalyst, which promotes this 'collective Self' to which the 'individual Self' also belongs. At this stage, one may say *"I am the Absolute and that thou art."* When this happens in an enormous manner, the differentiating quality of the individual becomes more and more flashed with the universality of fundamental existence, subsistence, and value, and then one is no longer tyrannized with the congenital idiosyncrasies of the person concerned.

It is a purification which can ultimately result in the effacing of the 'Self' and the 'other.' In yoga there is no duality. Here we feel the triple absence of individuation – the perceiver, the perceived, and the act of perception. Where the seer, the sight, and the seen are not known separately, where the heart has achieved the undisturbed depth of the silent spirit, there the yoga is achieved.

The Yogi enjoins upon himself the disciplines of five injunctions and five restraints. The five injunctions are deliberations to exercise. They are: to keep mind, word, actions, body, food, environment, and company clean; to engage in activities that promote serenity and joyfulness; to have programs of self-learning; to carry out the instructions of the preceptor; and to offer service to promote the welfare of the world. The restraints are to refrain: from causing hurt to any sentient being; from the fabrication of lies; from theft; from misappropriation; and from erroneous steps in the path of chastity.

Management Concepts of *Yoga Darśanam*

[VISION OF UNION]

(The Ability to Keep Union)

"United We Stand; Divided We Fall."

– U.S Propaganda Poster from World War II

It is the Vision of Union. In other words, it is the ability to keep 'Transpersonal Union,' so that, this can also be pronounced as 'Vision of Transpersonal Union.'

The word '*Yoga*' is derived from the Sanskrit term *"Yuj"* which means "to connect". *Yoga* is a connection of the human soul with the supreme soul. And such a spiritual union empowers a human to overcome lust, anger, and ego and live a virtuous life with spiritual awareness and compassion.

The Moon will wax and wane, the Sun will rise and set, the Earth will rotate…, the yogi will lead a life of piety. He will be in union with the Absolute. 'Action' is his mantra. *Nobody can remain even for a short while without engage in action,* says *Bhagavad Gita.* Yoga is a way of life. It involves *satvik* diet, positive thinking, spiritual study, health relationships, silent meditation, and selfless service.

Yoga, here, means union – the joining of two things – the mind and body. There are two types of unions – 'Intrapersonal Union' and 'Interpersonal Union.' Intrapersonal union is the union of mind and body of one person. Interpersonal union is the union between two persons.

Freudian School visualises 'Id', 'Ego', and 'Superego' as the causes of disunity and discords. Love is universally experienced as a process in which an effort of union is happening by providential grace. The real problem in the society stems from the disharmony between two hearts or two minds. The arch cause of interpersonal disharmony and disunity lies in intrapersonal discord. The interpersonal disunity is caused by intrapersonal discord. The 'Id', 'Ego', and 'superego' cause intrapersonal heterogeneity. Where there is 'ego', there the universal values such as love, compassion, justice, truth, merit etc shall find an exit., As against this, the universal values viz., love, compassion, justice, or truth is to create an inner cohesion and unity at the interpersonal level. A great alchemy that the Guru suggests, here, is 'True Love'. It is the Divine Love, the 'Benevolent Love' that can inter-relate persons through a process of fusing their interests. Love is universally experienced as a process in which an effort of union is made through conscious aspiration and an effortless union is happening by 'Providential Grace.' The sum and substance of *Yoga Darśanam* is such a beautiful incidence in which the knowledge of togetherness – of being one and identical – is complemented by the Guru. It is the sum total of the preparedness to live in amity. In yoga, in fine, there is no duality. "*I am the Absolute, That thou art*" (*aham brahma asmi, tat twamasi*).

Shalln't be, in a very plain thought, the intrinsic meaning of '*aham brahma asmi, tat twamasi*' is "*One Caste, One Religion, and One God for Mankind*"? Can't this arch slogan coined by

Guru remain as the pass word for 'Interpersonal Harmony?' *"When this happens in an enormous and continuous manner, the differentiating quality of the individual becomes more and more flushed with the universality of fundamental existence, subsistence, and value, and then one is no longer tyrannized with the congenital idiosyncrasies of the person concerned".*[1]

That which always unites and gets united is praised as yoga, as said earlier. In a world full of minute-to-minute provocations and nerve-wrecking anxieties, Yoga is the best panacea as a tool for 'Intrapersonal' union. It unites the body, soul, and spirit. There is no duality in Yoga. There is total concentration. Concentration – when it is simple, spontaneous, total, and not rebounding in reaction – is called the 'equipoise of the reasoning Self'. **The Yoga aims at concentration: "concentration of five senses; concentration of five operations; concentration on five forms of objectified sense contacts; concentration on five varieties of interests; and concentration on the five forms of vital energies."** The head-and-heart convention (universal convention) must take place through Yoga. When the heart, which is said to be the seat of ego, has known the undisturbed depth of the silent spirit, Yoga is achieved. When this is achieved, one cuts across all forms of phenomenality and gains the transparency of yogic vision. Then he says, *"All this is Brahma"* (*"sarvam khalvidam brahma."*). The word *Brahma,* meaning the Absolute, stands for *sama* (unitive).

The yogic discipline is goal oriented; it is always flowing. The final goal of a yogi is '*kaivalya* ', the primeval, unadulterated state of pure 'be-ness' and all acts of cognition, volition, and states of affection are aligned to achieve this goal. A contented businessman merges well his mind in the Absolute. When this is achieved, he cuts across all forms of phenomenality and gains the transparency of yogic vision. Then he says:

"sarvam Khalvidam Brahma"(all this is Brahma). The Yogic businessman sets the *kaivalya,* the primeval and unadulterated state of pure 'be-ness' as his ultimate goal. As every step is to be directed to progress towards the attainment of it, all acts of cognition, volition, and states of affection are to be aligned with his basic goal. His goal has to be both ontological and teleological. It is ontological because there is an approximation of the goal to a certain degree, and it is teleological because it refers to a future possibility.

In this hectic world, the state of ego (of businessman) has to be equipped with the right orientation to the goal – through perpetuating love, compassion, fellowship, and cheerfulness. Fearlessness is the foundation of supreme truth. It leads a businessman to be environment-friendly which will bind a harmony between business and environment. A unilateral posture of love in a situation of aggression and hatred can turn the situation. But the question that haunts the human mind is "to be or not to be?"

Guru was a conservationist. Guru's religion was fundamentally the "Religion of Ecology." He promoted compassion towards all living beings. Caring all living beings, tending, protecting, and serving them was his caste. It entails universal friendliness, forgiveness, and fearlessness. It leads to actions that have great relevance to contemporary environmental concerns. Human beings possess rationality and intuition. As a highly evolved form of life, they have a moral responsibility in their mutual dealings and in their relationship with the rest of the universe.

Through the *Yoga Darśanam*, Guru teaches us to be minimalists. Minimalists are happier with less of everything. – less wealth, fewer assets, less number of gadgets, less or no luxuries, less ego, less consumption, and no excesses. Western cultural standards are really a symbol of maximalism.

Most western countries and their leaders do not believe that there is only a fixed pie. Maximum production, maximum consumption, maximum emission...turning irresponsible towards the environment and future generations. This is the reason for the outrage of the 16-year-old teen activist girl from Sweden – Greta Thunberg – at the UN Climate Summit. In her short address starting **"How dare You?..."** asked the assembled Country Heads (on Tuesday, September 24, 2019, at UN H.Qs New York), and warned them: **"If you choose to fail us, I say we will never forgive you."**

The Guru was a galvanising force to transform the world from a mass of believers to individuals who seek the truth of life and beyond – "a shift from religion to responsibility." All conflicts in the world are essentially one man's belief vs. another man's belief. The moment one believes something, he becomes blind to everything else. A right belief system needs a flock; if and when we apply intelligence, our belief system will collapse. We shall be seekers, not believers. **"WE MEET HERE NOT TO ARGUE AND WIN, BUT TO KNOW AND TO BE KNOWN"** was the canon of love raised by Guru, at the International Religious Congress (*sarva matha sammelanam*) held at Aluva, in Kerala, in February 1924. Believing is assuming something unscientifically, without any clues. It provides confidence without clarity and proof; it is disastrous. It gives some imaginary heaven to the believers and it guides them blindly to the end they know nothing sure about. On the other hand, when we seek, we strive; we acquire phenomenal ability to create. Seekers strive and believers fight, though not generally established. When we strive, we create; when we fight, we destroy. *"Believers seek the Pie in the sky; the seekers seek the pie on the earth."*

A Yogi is always a seeker, and so it be a successful entrepreneur. "Only meditation and enlightenment takes the business yogi to the root of problems. In fact, meditation means revolution, for it goes and seeks problems at the radical level of thoughts. It is a journey of self-discovery, a journey within." It is a canon of success for philanthropic business personalities from East or West, North or South.

Guru's philosophy of *"One Caste, One Religion, and One God for Mankind"* is a basic social principle for cohesion and unity, and if followed, it would contribute significantly to alleviate the religious dis-order in the world. It may come in tandem with the Smithian notion of "human nature motivated by self-interests," (*"It is not from the benevolence of the butcher, the brewer, or the baker, that we expect our dinner, but from their regard to their own self-interest"* – Adam Smith), or the Darwian philosophy of "Natural Selection," (*Natural Selection or the preservation of favoured races in the struggle for life*" – Charles Darwin), or even the Marxian thesis of "Natural Antagonism" (*"Natural Antagonism between Capital and Labour"* – Karl Marx). Above all, Guru was a Gandhian too in Truth and Non-violence. There shall not be more vital a business philosophy for business community across the world than the Guru – Gandhian philosophy.

Guru raised a protective hedge around humanity, warding off the religious sentiments. Everyone is trying to live out his own life, and hence there are differences and clashes sometimes. Yet we are one and must co-exist. Some are violent, some untruthful, some greedy and some selfish. We are navigators and as we navigate life, we engage with all sorts of people. It is, indeed, difficult to remain non-violent in the face of violence, humbled in the face of ego, truthful in the face of untruth, selfless in the face of selfishness, and pure in the face of impurity. There are numerous interruptions and distractions. Amongst all these oddities, Guru pronounces *"Avanavan aatmasughathinn-*

acharikkunnava, Apārannu Sughthinayi Varenam." Guru seeks an economic order, alternative to the capitalist or communist fervour, and finds a social order. He advocated not individual highhandedness; instead he advised people to unite and taught that **"Union is Strength."** It is nothing else but a **"Collective Socialism."** A promising business leader promotes 'Collective Socialism' in his Organisation. Collective Socialism in business is the synonym of **'Participative Management.'** It is the sum and substance of *Yoga Darśanam*; it is the Social Order that the Guru envisaged. Hence, *Yoga Darśanam*, in Management Language, is *"The Theory of Collective Socialism," (or "The Theory of Participative Management").*

Sree Narayana Guru puts across two specific variances – *'anya'* and *'sama'. Anya* is negative and *sama* is positive. *Anya* is centrifugal and fissiparous, whereas *sama* is integrating and binding, and it creates a universal brotherhood and oneness. When and where the *'sama'* comes in action, there we see the birth of yoga. When this is achieved, one cuts across all forms of phenominality and gains the transparency of yogic vision. Then, all this is Brahma, *sarvam khalvidam Brahma*. The *sama* concept or the *sama bhavana* of Guru shall be the pendant on the necklace for socially responsible business magnates.

A yogic businessman endlessly promotes his capacity to both reconnoitre the situation and to direct all energies involved to continue the unbroken attention given to a chosen set of values and love. The yogic discipline of a leader sets an unadulterated state of pure 'be-ness'. He sees only love in the organisation. He attunes himself so as to tide over hatred and rivalry. He has his assigned niche in a given situation and he knows-shows-and goes the way. The yogic leader enjoins upon himself the disciplines of five injunctions and five restraints, as the Buddhists describe, says Guru. The five injunctions are deliberations to exercise. They are:

1. to keep mind, word, actions, body, food, environment and company clean;

2. to engage in activities that promote security and joyfulness;

3. to have programmes of self-learning;

4. to carry out the instructions of the preceptor; and

5. to offer service to promote the welfare of the world.

And the five restraints are the 'don'ts to refrain from,' viz.,:

1. causing hurt to any sentient being;

2. fabrication of lies;

3. theft;

4. misappropriation; and

5. erroneous steps in the path of chastity.

Guru, like Gandhiji, was for business ethics. Ethics are moral values, sensitivity, and sense of responsibility towards society. Ernest Hemingway said, *"I know only that what is moral is what you feel good after and what is immoral is what you feel bad after."*[2] Justice, truth, fairness, charity, and generosity are the dispositions of ethics that the Guru taught. They are the positives that one feels good after. As Spinoza rightly says, *"No one neglects anything which he judges to be good, except with the hope of gaining a greater good."*[3] Nobody leaves organisation with ethics but for a better option. Ethics are not rules based on laws; rather ethics are based on goodness. 'Goodness-in-action-mode' is ethics. Don't hurt, steal, or lie, and do unto others as you would have done unto you. It is Self-transformation.

By providing people more job autonomy and social support, enterprises can create healthier work places that are less stressful and eliminate the rising costs related to stress. Studies reveal that nearly half of India's private sector employees suffer from depression, anxiety, and stress. Demanding work schedules, high pressures for achieving the company's objectives and the always-on mobile phone syndrome are the top three culprits here. Management toxicity is affecting any employee more and more and they fall the pray to diabetic and cardio ailments. India is the world capital of these two diseases and they catch their preys 99 per cent in their 30s and 40s. More job autonomy and social support are the two saviours here. The problem of micro management is a menace and a sin as well. Let workers have job autonomy. Toxic work environment, forced ranking, 'grading-on-the-curve,' performance review, informal competition, transactional approaches and so on may recoil, many-a-time. May our Managers and Leaders listen to it?

[Recapitulation: (INTERPERSONAL HARMONY) The binding force of an Organisation is Love and Interpersonal Harmony. Yoga makes good cognitive deficit and it abridges inter-personal chasms. May our Businessmen listen to Rabindranath Tagore: "Be a human and a humane, a fully developed personality."]

Yoga Darśanam

1. Nitya Chaitanya Yati, (1987), *"The Psychology of Darśanasmala"*, Gurukula Publishing Hiuse, Fernhill – Varkala – Bainbridge, p.396, para 2.

2. Hemingway, Earnest., (1932), *"Death in the Afternoon,"* Simon and Schuster, New York, America.

3. Dutch Philosopher, Baruch Spinoza, *en.m.wikipedia.org.*

Chapter 10

NIRVĀNA DARŚANAM

Meaning:

The two events which are an absolute certainty in life are birth and death. In one sense, the entire life is a preparation for the final departure. The burning out of the phenomenal mark of individuation is termed as *'NIRVĀNA.'*

Nirvānā is of two kinds – the *pure* and the *impure*. That which is the *pure* is devoid of *'vāsana';* that is *impure* which conjoined with *'vāsana.' 'Vāsana'* means a past impression in mind that influences our behaviour and action.

Nirvānā means "burning out" or "extinction". *Nirvānā* is sometimes compared to a roasted seed that no longer has the potential to sprout. It is the union with the Absolute. From thereon there is no role to play, no programme to be fulfilled, and no mount to be ascended. That state is called *'Nirvriti.'* There is no wellbeing higher than this to achieve. So it is called *'Sreyas.'* It is like a piece of iron sucked into a magnetic field where the iron and the magnet become the same. Because of this quality, *Nirvānā* is called *'Brahma-samsparsa'*. *Brahma* means the Absolute; *Samsparsa* means to be actively in contact. Thereafter, the status of the individual is only nominal. *Nirvānā* is equated with *amrta*, immortality. And such a state of perfection is glorified as *'purnam'.*

It is the state of return to the source. As *Nirvānā* is equated with *'amrta'*, means 'immortality', such a state of perfectionism is glorified as *purnam*. Thus the union with the Absolute" can be *'suddha Nirvāna'* (pure extinction), *'ati suddha Nirvāna'* (more pure extinction), *'ati suddhatara Nirvāna'* (even more pure extinction), and *'ati suddhatama Nirvāna'* (the most pure extinction).

Those who become established in these four quarters can be respectively named as *'Brahmavit'* (the knower of the Absolute), *'Brahmavidvarta'* (superior in the knowledge of the Absolute), *'Brahmavidvariya'* (the more supreme in the knowledge of the Absolute), and *'Brahmavidvaristha'* (the most superior in the knowledge of the Absolute). The one Brahma alone is without a second, thus the knower should liberate from duality. Thereafter he does not return.

The wise one is not born, nor dies. 'This one has not come from anywhere, has not become anyone; this one is unborn, constant, eternal, and primeval. It is not slain when the body is slain. Water cannot wet it; sword cannot wound it: air cannot lighten it; and fire cannot burn it.'

The wise and the good of the world are turning it continuously from falsehood to truth, ignorance to knowledge, and exploitation to conservation. The seeker becomes a seer. The wise is one who is able to see action in inaction and inaction in action. That man's works are all devoid of desire and wilful motive. He relinquishes attachment to works, and always is happy and independent'. He is free from all expectancy and free from possessiveness, in whom that un-wisdom in the Self has been destroyed. His mind is balanced in 'Sameness'; free from blemish, stabilised in reason, delusion-free and never rejoice on good befalling him, nor be disturbed by a mishap.

Management Concepts of *Nirvāna Darśanam*

[VISION OF EMANCIPATION]

(The Ability To Accept The Culmination.)

> *"I do not feel obliged to believe that the same God who has endowed us with sense, reason, and intellect has intended us to forgo their use."*

> **– Galileo**

NIRVĀNA Darśanam means 'Vision of Emancipation.' Another definition is 'Vision of Finale,' as it is the final stage event. A third connotation is 'Vision of Climax' as it expresses the apogee and climax of the total stages of growth.

In Hinduism and Buddhism, *Nirvāna* is the highest state that someone can attain, a state of enlightenment, a place of perfect peace and happiness – like heaven – where a person's individual desires and sufferings go away. The Sanskrit meaning of *'Nirvāna'* is "extinction", or "disappearance" of the individual to the universal entity. It is a place or state of complete bliss and delight and peace which is the final goal of Buddhism. Paradise, Heaven, Eden (*the Bible*), the Promised Land/the Land of Canaan (*the Bible*)[1], Elysium (*Greek mythology*),[2] Fantasy-land, Lotus-land, Never-never-land (*J.M.Barrie*),[3] Shangri-la (*James Hilton*),[4] New Jerusalem (*the Bible*), Utopia (*Sir Thomas More*),[5] Happy Valley, Zion (Sion) (*the Bible*) etc are the places where one's soul rest in peace after *Nirvāna*. The words related to the concept of *Nirvāna* are 'arcadia, dreamland, dream world, wonderland, blessedness, bliss, blissfulness, euphoria, gladness, joy, state of utter perfection and happiness.'

Lord Buddha compares Nirvāna to "the merging of a dewdrop into the infinitude of the ocean"; Jesus Christ compares it to "the return of a prodigal son to acknowledge the profound love and compassion of an all-knowing father".[6]

The Japanese Biologist, Yoshinori Ohsumi, Nobel Laureate in Physiology and Medicine, remarked in his Nobel Prize acceptance lecture in December 2016: *"Life is an equilibrium state between synthesis and degradation of proteins. Synthesis means creation, and degradation implies annihilation."* As long as vital organs are in equilibrium, there is life. Once these organs are stressed and disequilibrium sets, life becomes endangered. French Physiologist, Claude Bernard, opines, *"Stability of internal environment (in the body) is the condition for free and independent life."*[7] *The* Synthesis-Degradation balance sets equilibrium. A non-equilibrium state reads an imbalance between them.

In *Nirvāna Darśanam,* we shall take the positive interpretation of euphoria, blissfulness, gladness, happiness, and joy; we do not touch the negative connotation of extinction, disappearance, death or annihilation or obliteration. It is akin to "the Fifth Stage of Economic Growth" depicted by Walt Whitman Rostow.[8] The five stages of economic growth elucidated by Rostow in his classic growth model are *(1) The Traditional Society, (2)* The *Pre-conditions for Take-off, (3) The Take-off, (4) The Drive to Maturity, and (5) The Age of High Mass Consumption.* The *Nirvāna,* in the present context, is the fifth stage – 'The Age of High Mass Consumption'.

"It is the post-maturity stage: a well advanced industrial ambience; the balance of attention of the society is shifted from Supply to Demand, from problems of Production to problems of Consumption, and of welfare in the widest sense. The resources are diverted in pursuit of national power and world influence; the income is re-distributed to correct the aberrations of the market process; and there is an extension of Consumer Demand on durable consumer goods and high grade foods."

The 'Need Hierarchy'[9] of Abraham Maslow, the American psychologist, postulates five stages of Human Needs. The five needs are: *(1) Physiological Needs, (2) Safety Needs, (3) Belongingness and Love Needs, (4) Esteem Needs, and (5) Self Actualisation Needs.* Can we equate the last stage – Self Actualisation – to the *Nirvāna* Stage of Guru? Yes, we can. The last level of human motivation is "Self Actualisation" where all the additional (marginal) utility that comes from additional unit (of consumption) will be zero or even negative. Since then the theory of Diminishing Marginal Utility (DMU) sets in. It is the maximum growth level/motivation level, beyond which entrepreneurs go generous and become philanthropists. The ultra-wealthy business magnates like Jeff Bezos (Amazon, USA), Bill Gates (Microsoft, USA), Warren Buffett (Berkshire Hathaway, USA), Bernard Arnault (LVMH, France), Mark Zuckerberg (Face book, USA)......or Azim Premji (Wipro, India) – have reached this level of *Nirvāna.*

Surely, a question arises here: "will the last stage remain perennial and everlasting?".

No. Not at all.

Why?

Why, because, '**disruption**' is an inevitable factor in business. The passé must go, and the new must ring in. The 'Fourth Industrial Revolution' is already making deep inroads. The '**Digital Disruption**' is boundlessly marching ahead sweeping and ebbing away the existing knowhow and technologies raising the slogan that 'Learn, Un-learn, and Re-learn.' It is characterised by Machine-thinking and Artificial Intelligence (AI), plus VUCA (Volatility, Uncertainty, Complexity, and Ambiguity) syndrome. The **Disruptive Innovations** sweep across the world and various brands fall off cliff and get disappeared.

Tungabhadra Steel Products, Spice Trading Corporation of India, Bharat Jute, Hindustan Cables, Central Inland Water Transport Corporation, Hindustan Organic Chemicals, HMT Watches, National Jute Manufacturers Corporation, Tyre Corporation of India, Hindustan Photo Films Manufacturing etc are the public sector undertakings which are seriously sick and to be closed down or must be subject to re-engineering. Either the natural death (liquidation) or the revival plans are to be employed. The liquidation is *NIRVĀNA,* and the revival plans mean the *'Nirvāna Extended.'*

If the revival plans fail, it will come to a cessation. Safe landing is advisable and remarkably beautiful, and if it fails, the outcome shall be crash landing, belly landing, or landing on water bed. Whatever be said or sung, the *Nirvāna* stage will arrive at sooner or later to any business enterprise as in the case of natural beings of plant and animal kingdoms. *NIRVĀNA Darśanam* tells us the very truth that for anything and everything in the world will have a **culmination and a cessation.** So, *Nirvāna Darśanam* is *"The Theory of Culmination," (or "The Theory of Disruption").*

Wick burns till there is oil in the lamp; a candle burns only until there is no more wax left. A cessation stage for any skill is inevitable. A businessman or a business is no exception to this rule. Business organisations enter the scene, flourish, and getting wiped off from the scene. The entry and the exit are the two ends – the entry is *Perigee (perihelion)* and the exit is *Apogee (aphelion).*

The aeronautical metaphor of Rostow is an allegory or a parable mapping the take-off to landing of an airplane. 'The Age of High Mass Consumption' indicates the 'Auto-piloting' stage of an aircraft after reaching up its required altitude in the course of its flight. It is the most comfortable time for the aircraft, for its crew, and for the passengers and other pay-loads.

When the aircraft reaches its required altitude atop, the only and the only one option left is landing. Similarly, a business organisation will have a landing and grounding stage. It is the stage of liquidation, otherwise called the extinction. In certain cases a re-birth like amalgamation, absorption, re-structuring, re-engineering or cartelling or pooling is taken place, as the time is passing by.

On the physical and phenomenal mark of organisational entity, there may be two types of extinctions and one style of existence. These three states can be named as *Nirvriti, Nisreyas, and Sreyas.* They are the total stoppage of business; the merger with an existing company; and the vehement existence in the market, respectively. The following narrations may elucidate them:

Nirvriti: This category consists of companies which return to the source after the completion of the job undertaken. With the finale of the project, the company winds itself up and return to the source. Thereafter, there is no existence for the company and suspends itself its animation. The Management seeks another project(s) to start with and goes after the new project. A candle burns only until there is no more wax left to continue the process of oxidation. A new candle will not emerge from a burnt out one. The total satisfaction or fulfilment of the objectives of the company urges its exit as there is no role to play, no programmes to be fulfilled, no mount to be ascended. This ecstatic state of beatitude is called '*Nirvriti*', means boundlessness. There is no well-being higher than this to achieve. Thereafter, the status of the Organisation is only nominal and becomes a part of Commercial History.

Perigee and Apogee, East and West, Rise and Set, Wax and Wane ... are all absolute certainties. The Sun rises and sets, the Moon waxes and wanes, Stars shine and vanish, Trees blooms and disappear... it is the natural cyclic phenomenon. In a true sense, any phenomenon is a travel from beginning to the end. The cessation of activity and return to the source is inevitable. What happens in between is only the preparation for reaching the finale. After that...? After that it is 'ex *nihilo*', means, nothingness, or hollowness.

Nisreyas: The second category of companies finds a rescue under the umbrella of titanic existing companies as a merged entity with it. Merger, acquisition, absorption, amalgamation, and re-organisation are the various options here. Accepting any of these options loses its original identity and existence. For them, there is no 'well-being' higher than this to achieve. This final release from all motivations enables the management to transcend even the idea of well-being. Hence, this state is called '*Nisreyas.*' Here, the part is re-absorbed into whole. In the commercial world, an existing individual company is the part compared to the entire 'business galaxy.' "It is like a piece of iron sucked into a magnetic field where the iron and the magnet become the same." Guru says it as '*Brahma Samsparsa.*' '*Brahma*' means the Absolute; '*Samsparsa*' means to be actively in contact. Thereafter the status of the individual absorbed/merged company is only nominal and becomes the part of the existing whole.

Sreyas: The third category is equated with '*amartya*', the immortal. Such a state of perfection is glorified as '*purnam.*' There can be traces of success and continuous existence. There are varieties of experiential and imperiential pursuits for the company. Therefore it is called '*Sreyas.*' This may be the zenith of growth of a business. It is the stage of, as WW Rostow puts it, **'The Age of High Mass Consumption.'** It is the fifth and the last stage of the Aeronautical Metaphor of Economic Growth propounded by Walt Whitman Rostow in his theory, '*The Stages of Economic Growth.*

Between the first formation of clay and the final definitive culmination of it in to a well-baked usable pot, there is an unsung history of pains and stakes. At this stage, the business man is placed one degree below the most pure. There is not even the slightest stain of ego. So, he is included among the pure. He is the knower of the 'Self' and there shines wisdom Sun-like. Such a leader can be considered a *'Business Sanyasi'*, as well as one matured in the highest form of devotion and commitment, has no hatred but friendly and compassionate, free from possessiveness and in short a unitively-disciplined leader who is always contented, self-controlled, firmly resolved and fit in senses.

He plays the **'Blue Sky Strategies'** and the triple modalities of nature – *tamas, rajas, and satva* – do not any longer monitor his consciousness. Instead, at this stage, the business baron could convert his *tamas bhava* (quality of *tamas*) to *rajas bhava (quality of rajas)* so as to activate his *satva gunas to* lead and grow. The inner light is identical with the outer light. It is the first principle of luminosity. It is transcendental. It is the light of lights. It is the self luminous light of the 'Self.' However, at last, such a leader also will succumb to mortality, but his business will still exist based on the crown glory of the past, waiting for another leader to come. Arch example: Jamsetji Nusserwanji Tata, the legendary 'Father of Indian Industry' bequeathed his legacy to the Tata Group, India's biggest Conglomerate entity. It had been passed over through Dorabji Tata, JRD Tata, Ratanji Tata and now has been reached to the great-grandson Ratan Tata. Leaders will come and go as the time is passing by, yet the business remains in existence reminding the famous business canon of Dual Entity.

The legacy and the ancestral lineage descending from a rich pure-bred pedigree guarantees the homozygous for traits to run a company for centuries ahead as a glorious dynasty. The business genealogy transmutes 'lead' into 'Gold,' whereas, paternal deficit is a potent variable which drags down the business clan into quagmire and then to whirlpool of mismanagement and clutter and will experience the "Scylla-Charybdis" syndrome before the ultimate collapse. Toil, achieve, and maintain and fly atop through generations and keep the flag fluttering are the signs of **Blue Sky Strategy.** The vast infinite expanse of the Blue Sky is remaining very sensitive not only for Cosmonaut-Astronaut-Scientists, nor for Cosmologists, Meteorologists, or Poets, but for Business Ambassadors as well. *"I doubt we would last for next 1000 years – the Earth is facing that much catastrophes – but I hope, meanwhile we would reach the Stars,"* said Stephen William Hawking. The Sky is the ultimate rescue place cited by the great scientist. The victorious business chiefs advice others to 'aim at Sky' to grow economic pie.

The BCG Growth Share Matrix[10] depicts (a) **Question Mark,** (b) **Dog,** (c) **Cash Cow,** and (d) **Star,** in its four quadrants, and summarises that the Star is the Market Leader. **The Blue Sky Strategy** aims at Stars. The transformed meaning of NIRVĀNA *Darśanam* used in the present work is the total emancipation from all shackles to lead the Business Organisation to the 'Blue-Sky-Infinite' as an Immortal *Artificial Being Created by Law...* (Indebted to the definition of a 'Company' given in the Indian Companies Act), though the mortal owners disappear behind the great curtain of Nature in the course of time.

Sree Narayana Guru closes another of his books – *Atmopadesa Satakam* (One Hundred Verses of Self Instruction) – with a similar verse:

> *"Neither this, nor that, nor the content of existence am I,*
> *But existence, subsistence, joy-immortal; thus attaining clarity,*
> *Emboldened, discarding attachment to being and non-being,*
> *One should gently, gently, merge in SAT-AUM."* [11]

[Recapitulation: (CULMINATIVE AWARENESS) The Businessman must be aware of the Culmination and the End. Only a 'Business *Rishi'* can do that. He attains *Moksha* and his business still resumes serving under new leadership. And it shall be Star in the infinite expanse of the Blue Sky]

"AUM TAT SAT."

Nirvāna Darśanam

1. *The Hebrew Bible,* "Canaan, the land promised by God to Abraham and his descendants," Genesis 12:7.

2. The Greek Mythology, *"Elysian Fields, the home of the blessed after death."*

3. Barrie, James Matthew., (1953), *"Peter Pan,"* Scotland, pp.65–74.

4. Hilton, James., (1933), *"Lost Horizon,"* Macmillan Publishers, London, p.120.

5. Sir Thomas More, (1516), *"Utopia,"* More, London.

6. Nitya Chaitanya Yati, (1987), *"The Psychology of Darśanasmala"*, Gurukula Publishing Hiuse, Fernhill – Varkala – Bainbridge, p.430, para 2.

7. *Wikipedia.org*

8. Rostow, Walt Whitman., (1960), *"The Stages of Economic Growth: A Non Communist Manifesto"*, Cambridge University Press, pp 4–16.

9. Maslow, Abraham., (1943), *"A Theory of Human Motivation"* Essay, Psychological Review (journal), America.

10. *BCG Matrix*: The Boston Consulting Group's Product Portfolio Matrix, designed to help with long term strategic planning to decide where to invest, to discontinue or develop products.

11. Sree Narayana Guru, (1897), *"Atmopadesa Sathakam,"* verse 100.

SUM UP

To sum up, *The Darśana Mālā* of Sree Narayana Guru could be put up in a nutshell as:

ADHYĀROPA DARŚANAM	:	*VISION OF SUPPOSITION*
APAVĀDA DARŚANAM	:	*VISION OF TRUTH*
ASATYA DARŚANAM	:	*VISION OF NON-EXISTENCE*
MĀYĀ DARŚANAM	:	*VISION OF NEGATION*
BHĀNA DARŚANAM	:	*VISION OF AWARENESS*
KARMA DARŚANAM	:	*VISION OF ACTION*
JANA DARSANAN	:	*VISION OF CONSCIOUSNESS*
BHAKTI DARŚANAM	:	*VISION OF CONTEMPLATION*
YOGA DARŚANAM	:	*VISION OF UNION*
NIRVĀNA DARŚANAM	:	*VISION OF EMANCIPATION*

The *Darśanas* in their theoretical transformations can be read as:

ADHYĀROPA DARŚANAM: The Theory of Entrepreneurial Explosion (or The Theory of Entrepreneurial Trinity).

APAVĀDA DARŚANAM: The Theory of Gross-Subtle (Sthūla Suksma) Analysis (or The Theory of Root Cause Analysis).

ASATYA DARŚANAM: The Theory of Atma Vidya (or The Theory of Self Knowledge).

MĀYĀ DARŚANAM: The Theory of Noumenon and Phenomenon (or The Theory of Nescience and Science).

BHĀNA DARŚANAM: The Theory of Awareness (or The Theory of Conscious Management).

KARMA DARŚANAM: The Theory of Nishkama Karma (or The Theory of Undesirous Action).

JANA DARSANAN: The Theory of Transcendental Awareness (or The Theory of Self Management).

BHAKTI DARŚANAM: The Theory of Love, Devotion, Compassion, and Empathy or The Theory of Loyalty)).

YOGA DARŚANAM: The Theory of Collective Socialism (or The Theory of Participative Management).

NIRVĀNA DARŚANAM: The Theory of Culmination (or The Theory of Disruption).

In a very critical thought, the author equates these *Darśanas* to the renowned theory – **"The Stages of Economic Growth"** – propounded by the American Economist, Walt Whitman Rostow (1916–2003). The Rostowian Theory proposes Five Stages of Economic Growth for a country. Rostow argued that the economies of all countries could be placed within one of five different stages of economic growth. The stages are: **"Traditional Society, Pre-conditions for Take-off, Take-off, Drive to Maturity, and Age of High Mass Consumption."** As there are ten *Darśanas,* and/but there are only Five Stages in the Rostowian Theory, the author takes the liberty to coin five more stages using the prefix 'Pre' to each Stage of Rostow's theory so as to suit to the Ten *Darśanas* quite well in fit. Thus the modified ten concepts are:

(1) **(Pre-Traditional Society), Traditional Society,**

(2) **(Pre-Pre-Conditions for Take Off), Pre-Conditions for Take-Off,**

(3) (Pre-Take-Off), Take-Off,

(4) (Pre-Drive to Maturity), Drive to Maturity, and

(5) (Pre-Age of High Mass Consumption), Age of High Mass Consumption.

The newly coined five stages are bracketed for easy readability and comprehension. As commented Rostow in his Growth Model that an economy passes through the various stages in its upward growth, a Business Organisation (a Start-up) goes through the ten stages mentioned above, in its life span. The ten *Darśanas* of Guru, in their respective Vision Concepts and Theoretical Aspects, guide the Start-up enterprise in its growth path and the novice businessman's thoughts will be influenced and directed by these *Darśanas* which manifest as milestones in his journey from the beginning 'Supposition (*ADHYĀROPA)* to final Emancipation (*NIRVĀNA*).'

For comprehension and to make it easy to understand, the author endeavours here to pair up ten *Darśanas* of *Darśana Mālā* into five pairs, so that, they can be equated to the Five Stages of Economic Growth summarised by WW Rostow, or the five Human Needs in the rhythmic linear order, developed by the American Psychologist, Abraham Maslow in his 'Need Hierarchy.'

1. *(a) Adhyāropa Darśanam* **(The Theory of Entrepreneurial Explosion)** is Vision of Supposition as its content is the superimposition. It is also called 'Vision of Super-imposition' or 'Vision of Cosmic Projection.' This superimposition is, many-a-time, far away from the truth and reality. It is like a flight of fancy. Any new-comer in business world would swim in the sea of supposition as a premature novice. At this primitive stage, the guiding principle is the 'Vision of Supposition' and the Organisation

suffers as machinery used are crude, the labour unskilled, capital poor, and the organisational part is rudimentary. To make a simile of Walt Whitman Rostow's Economic Growth Model, this stage can be coined as **'Pre-Traditional Society.'**

(b) *Apavāda Darśanam* (The Theory of Root Cause Analysis) is 'Vision of Non-Supposition.' It is also called 'Vision of Truth' – 'Vision of Truth by Constant Refutation of the False.' The 'beaten-businessman-the-novice' slowly recognises his faults and getting ready for a change of course-of-actions and move towards the next stage of growth.' Here, he consistently struggles for correcting falsehoods and faults for survival. He recognises and distinguishes the 'Rope and Snake.' Ignorance and darkness get away slowly. The initial symptoms of growth appear, the business entity starts moving ahead. However, still the Organisation is in its primitive stage and it is akin to the stage of *'Traditional Society'* concept of W. W. Rostow.

[Recapitulation: The entrepreneur is the Brahma-Vishnu-Maheswara of his enterprise. Passing through the above two stages, he thinks only about the genesis of his business just as a Start-Up and his thoughts and being are subject to errors of omissions (actus reus) and commissions (error of inadvertence). The superimposition of thoughts plus nescience and ignorance make him deaf, dumb and crippled. And the Business Organisation under his command would be a lame duck. Pulling and pushing, puffing and panting the Start-Up gets crawled in its upward movement. These are the symptoms of "Traditional Society."]

2. **(a) *Asatya Darśanam* (The Theory of *Atmavidya*)** is 'Vision of Non-existence.' It says that man lives in the woeful condition of ignorance. He doesn't know what is real and what is unreal. As Matthew Arnold laments in his poem *Dover Beach*...

"And we are here as on a darkling plain
Swept with confused alarms of struggle and flight,
Where ignorant armies clash by night."

Guru proposes *atmavidya* (knowledge of *atma* or Self) as a panacea to get rid of the evil effects of ignorance and *tamas*. It will guide the entrepreneur through vicissitudes and the business starts registering progress in science and technology. When the 'businessman-the-beginner' learns *atmavidya* to realise the 'Real' from the 'Un-real', he reaches the primary stage of the third level of Rostowian growth, say, *'Pre-Pre-Conditions for Take-off.'*

(b) Māyā Darśanam (**The Theory of Noumenon and Phenomenon**) is the 'Vision of Negation' and also called 'Vision of Non-being Beingness.' It is a critical study of both the noumenon and the phenomenon. In the previous *Darsana,* Guru gave us the efficient method for the discernment of the real from the unreal. In this *Darsana,* he gives directions to discern the truthful basis of superimpositions of falsehood. Negation means denial. We must deny the untruth and falsehood and take our mind away from non-being beingness. The negative factors conceal truth from us. The entrepreneur must have a correct perception of the empirical world and its transactional verity. Through *atmavidya* he attains new impetus. The Vision of Negation guides the businessman through self-sustaining and normal growth. It can be related to the *'Pre-Conditions for Take-off'* stage of the Rostowian Model of economic growth.

[Recapitulation: The Asatya Darśanam and MĀYĀ Darśanam, in unison, takes the business into the next level of progress, say, the "Pre-Conditions for Take Off." The entrepreneur passes through the stage of ignorance but he is happened to learn atmavidya to realise the 'Real' from the 'Unreal.' By a continuous negation,

he evades untruth and falsehood and he equips himself with the marvels of science and technology and gets himself prepared for the next remarkable growth path of "Pre-Take Off," the prelude of "Take Off."]

3. **(a) Bhāna Darśanam (The Theory of Conscious Management)** is Vision of Awareness. *BHĀNA* means basic consciousness. In this *Darśanam,* Guru makes us familiar with the sixteen aspects of the altering states of awareness in between the main two categories – Generic and Specific awareness. The sum and substance of these sixteen varied aspects of consciousness is nothing else but 'Self Awareness.' This Self Awareness is the *sine-qua-non* for a successful business man. The greatest awareness is the awareness of the Self. It is the awareness of awarenesses. The well awared organiser will amass sources for expansion and sophistication. By doing it, the business will reach its *'Pre*-Take-off' stage.

(b) Karma Darśanam **(The Theory of *Nishkama Karma*)** is 'Vision of Action.' It is otherwise called 'Vision of Cosmo-psychological Functionalism.' In Sanskrit, action is called *karma.* Every form of transaction in our transactional world has within it the dynamics of action. Every action of a wise man contains within itself a quality of love and consideration. Such a man is in harmony with universal Self. The actions of one who is wise are unitive and resonate with wisdom. An entrepreneur of wisdom and truth would succeed in his undesirous actions. He will attract his men and his magnetism will ensure *esprit de corps in the Organisation.* And it will create normal and self sustaining growth to the business. At this level, the Organisation gains a new vigour and dynamism and the enterprise enjoys its much awaited *'Take-off.'*

[Recapitulation: On reaching this state of affairs, the basic consciousness of the business leader develops much and he attains the Generic and Specific realms of awareness well. The Self Awareness backed by Nishkama Karma supports him vehemently in his onward march for branding the business and its merchandise. The Business Takes-Off and registers an indelible mark in the market.]

4. *(a) Jñāna Darśanam* (**The Theory of Transcendental Awareness**) is 'Vision of Consciousness.' To be clearer, it is the vision of Consciousness and its Modifications. It is called *atma Jñāna* in Sanskrit. It means knowledge of 'Self Realization.' It is also called knowledge of the non-Self. Self Realisation is the true knowledge of Self and when it manifests, then onwards starts wisdom and practical experience. Through *atmavidya* and *atma Jñāna* the businessman attains 'Self Awareness' and 'Self Consciousness.' His leadership qualities could have attained transcendental inputs. The business makes its imprint in the society and the products get branded. The Self-Realisation motivates the owner, so that, a new boost emerges to take the business to its stage of *'Pre-Drive to Maturity.'*

(b) Bhakti Darśanam (**The Theory of Love, Devotion, Compassion and Empathy**) is 'Vision of Contemplation.' It is vividly called 'Vision of Contemplative Devotion'. Love, devotion, compassion, empathy, and consequent rapture of mind occur spontaneously rather than as mechanical discipline. Such feelings are named *'actus purus'* which means pure action, in English. It is in this pure joy that one experiences one's natural alignment with the Absolute. It is possible through a continuous contemplation of one's Self. The highly motivated and successful

business tycoon would climb new heights and maintains it provided he perpetuates Love, Devotion, Compassion, and Empathy. The fame of the business and businessman crosses national borders. Now it is a multinational being. It is the stage of *'Drive to Maturity.'*

[Recapitulation: The dichotomy of Jñāna-Bhakti Darśanams pushes up the business in its vertical growth. The business Baron, having learned atmaJñāna along with atmavidya realises the basics of 'Transcendental Leadership.' It gets momentum when the 'Vision of Contemplation' (Vision of Love) adds its impetus and he shoots up into the sky of business like an aircraft climbs up to its required altitude where it would be free of gravitational pull of the Earth. This level of growth is the Rostowian concept of "Drive to Maturity."]

5. *(a) Yoga Darśanam* (**The Theory of Collective Socialism**) is 'Vision of Union', better called 'Vision of Transpersonal Union.' Yoga is otherwise called 'Union' and it suggests the joining of two or more things. The real problem stems from disunion and disharmony and the answer to such a primary problem is union and the resultant harmony. The root cause of interpersonal disunity lies in intrapersonal discord. The Organisation would be heard for its growth and 'Participative Management.' It is free from intrapersonal heterogeneity and stays in amity altogether. There is no duality. The learned business Magnate stands tall in the business world where only few rivals remain. And the business is said to be in its enviable growth stage named *'Pre-Age of High Mass Consumption.'*

(b) Nirvāna Darśanam (**The Theory of Culmination**) is 'Vision of Emancipation.' It is the 'Vision of Finale.' It can also be

defined as 'Vision of Climax.' In essence, it is the process of contemplative absorption of the individualised personal Self in the totality of the universal Self. It is the final exit. In business terms, it is the zenith of growth path. The business would have become a 'Star' in business horizon and its products/services would be known globally. The visionary business Boss enjoys the commanding heights in world scenario. At this stage he is braver than he believes, stronger than he seems, and smarter than he thinks. The spontaneous bliss of uninterrupted Self knowledge and personal cum commercial wisdom would take him to the unsurpassed fame and glory. To make a simile of Rostowian Model, it is the last stage of growth-path – *'Age of High Mass Consumption.'*

[Recapitulation: *Yoga Darśanam* teaches the magic of 'Vision of Union' and the relevance of harmony and 'Participative Management.' The Organisation will be heard for its growth and unity. *Nirvāna Darśanam* (the Vision of Emancipation) helps the business CEO to be free from all clutches plus ego and Self motives and the visionary transcendental leader goes up to the zenith to assume the attire of *'Leader Immanent.''* And, at this stage of growth, the Business Organisation enjoys the bliss of 'Auto-Piloting' where there is no limit except the vast serenity of horizon in its blue infinite expanse.]

In fine, as an epilogue, we can pretty confidently brief that the businessman is the *Brahma-Vishnu-Mahesawara* of his business. Beginning as a Start-Up at a very rudimentary and modest level, he struggles for existence and subsistence, acquires truth, learns to separate the Real from the Unreal through *Sthūla-Sooksma nireekshan*, learns *atmavidya* and *atmaJñāna* to attain Generic-Specific Self Awareness, engages in *Nishkama Karma* and Takes-Off himself and his business, practices Self-Realisation so that learns the science of Contemplation and love which lead him to Yoga the Union and Participation in the Organisation and all these forces together elevate him up into the world of Emancipation where he witnesses his business in High Altitude of "Age of High Mass Consumption." It is the Course of the *'Blue Sky Strategy.'*

At this realm the "Business Man-Business-Quality" will be 9,9 (i.e., at the zenith) as depicted in the following "Business Man-Business-Quality-Matrix" (borrowed the *Blake-Mouton Model*).

The Managerial Grid Model (1964) is a style of Leadership Model developed by Robert R. Blake and Jane Mouton – both were the American Management Theoreticians – to measure the Leader's "Concern for People" vs. "Concern for Production." Now, here we can borrow the Model as it is, or with a change of measuring the "Leadership Traits" vs. "Individual (Personal) Traits" of a CEO.

"Business Man-Business-Quality-Matrix."

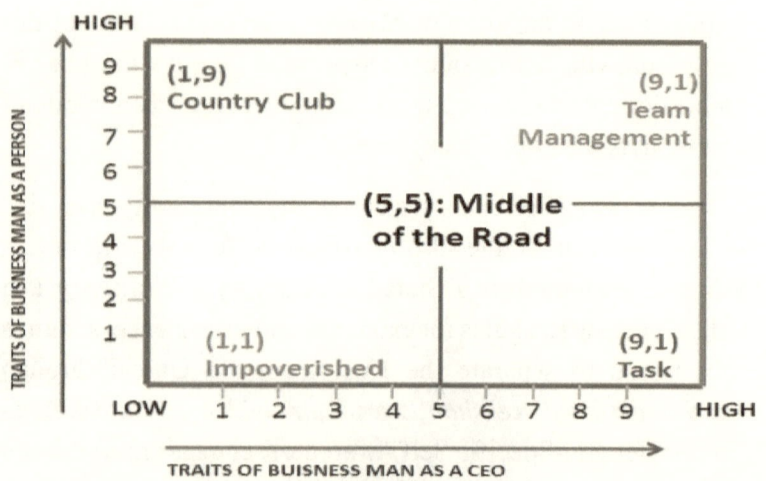

The OX axis measures (0 – 9 single-digit-scale) the Leadership Traits and the OY axis measures (0 – 9 single-digit-scale) his Individual (Personal) Traits, as a citizen.

The Indifferent (Impoverished style) Leader is 1,1 Leader;
The Accommodating (Country-club style) Leader is 1,9 Leader;
The Dictatorial (Produce or Perish style) Leader is 9,1 Leader;
The Status quo (Middle-of-the-road style) Leader is 5,5 Leader; and
The Sound (Team Leader style) Leader is 9,9 Leader.

The Sound (Team Leader) CEO puts himself and his business at the 'pith-and-the-zenith' glory. If we borrow W.W. Rostow, the Leader and his Business will be at "The Age High of Mass Consumption"; to borrow Abraham Maslow, the Boss and his Organisation will be at its "Self Actualisation Stage"; when we hire BCG Growth Matrix, the Leader and the Led would be "Stars" in the Business Sky.

Learning 'Supposition' from *Addhyaropa Darśanam;* 'Sthūla – Sūksma Comprehension' from *Apavāda Darśanam;* '*atmavidya*' from *Asathya Darśanam;* 'Nescience-Science' from *Māyā Darśanam;* 'Self-Awareness' from *Bhāna Darśanam;* '*Nishkama Karma*' from *Karma Darśanam;* 'Transcendentalism' from *Jñāna Darśanam;* 'Contemplation' from *Bhakti Darśanam;* '*esprit-de-corps*' from *Yoga, Darśanam* and 'Culmination' from *Nirvāna Darśanama,* 'the-once-a-novice-leader' has now grown up to the level of "Star-a-CEO," and his Enterprise the "Moon" in the Sky.

To sum up, the ***Darśana Mālā*** of Jagat-Guru Sree Narayana Gurudevan could be appellated as *"**The Blue Sky Strategy**"* for Business and Businessman. It is an "**Epiphany of Management Thoughts.**"

Part Three

EPILOGUE

(Part A)

The Guru Effect

A Right Seer At The Right Time At The Right Place:

The birth, the being, and the words and the deeds of the Guru remind us: *"yada yada hi dharmasya*

> *glanir bhavathi bharatha*
> *abhyuthanam adharmasya*
> *tadatmanam srjamy aham*
>
> *paritrayana sadhunam*
> *vinasaya ca duskritam......*
> *dharma sansthapanarthaya*
> *sambhavaami yuge yuge". (Bhagavat Gita, chapter IV,*
> *verses 7 & 8.)*

"Whenever and wherever there is decline of righteousness and a rise of
Unrighteousness......For the protection of the good,
For the destruction of the wicked, and
For the establishment of righteousness, I am born in every age".

The physical environment, the chemistry of the social milieu, the outlook of people, the culture, the ethos... everything in the social fabric of the Nation was caste-based and colour-oriented and retarding the balanced growth. The society was crippled, numbed, and totally fatigued and torn – then, akin to the verse of

Gita, – the Country witnessed the birth of the baby (Guru). 'The Baby was born at the Right Place, at the Right Time', so as to lead the society through the ages and to be transmuted himself into a Leader.

The caste system in Kerala reminds us an analogy of a 'canine training centre.' A fence of wire around to guard the dogs in; they get trained in it; the fence is removed in the later stage of training, but the dogs are so conditioned that they keep themselves in the area, not getting beyond it. Similarly, the ugly caste system and un-touchability were barbed wire fences in Indian society which kept people in water-tight compartments. Even years after, the lower castes keep themselves away from the common scenes afraid of the invisible fences of caste, creed, and un-touchabiltiy.

The deprived and the down-trodden populace were organised and motivated by the Guru and led them to the limelight of education, agriculture, arts, festivals, industry, commerce, and employment. It is the "Transcendental Leadership". In a common parlance, it was the "Management of Masses". And the Guru transformed himself in to the position of 'Manager of Humanity' and became the 'Leader of the lesser-breeds.'

*"In India every region has had its galaxy of wisdom teachers, poets and singers – from **Jnaneswara** in the Maharastra west to **Ramakrishna** in the Bengal East and from **Guru Nanak** in the Punjab north to **Narayana Guru** in the Kerala south. Some like **Sankara, Ramanuja, and Madhva**, have emerged from the orthodox fold of Vedic Brahminism; others such as **Thiruvalluvar** or **Thukaram** and also **Narayana Guru**, from primarily non-Vedic, pre-Aryan backgrounds; while others such as the **Buddhist** and **Jaina**, have represented heterodox approaches"* (Prof. Ramachandra Guha, "A *response to certain references to the Guru, gurunarayanalokam.com*).

Guru, the Unreasonable One:

"The reasonable man adapts himself to the world; the unreasonable one persists in trying to adapt the world to himself. Therefore, all progress depends on the unreasonable man." [George Bernard Shah, (1901), *"Man and Superman"*]. Yes, it is true. All progress depend on the unreasonable man. Great thinkers, seers, and gurus were/are there in and around; they were/are strong on the thinking process, but weak on the execution side. Ideation, no matter how big, assumes value when it is acted upon and brought to life. Otherwise, it may remain as a diamond in rough, unnoticed. The unreasonable Guru put in his faithful service to emancipate the downtrodden and the deprived masses from the yoke of casteism and discrimination.

The caste system in Kerala was so rigid that Swami Vivek Ananda qualified the State of Kerala as "Lunatic Asylum". The social rights and privileges were concentrated and enjoyed by the so-called upper castes only. No temple entry, no right for education, and no road commuting right for the lower castes.

"No one is high and no one is low; according to one's virtues and vices one is happy, miserable, rich, or poor, or one is a fool, and another is erudite, but all are fundamentally human beings. And every living being is part of *Brahman* or universal consciousness" – says Guru. This 'Theory of Oneness' rules the roost, today. Can the modern world pronounce it as **"Management Theory of Oneness"**?

Creative ideas do not spring from groups, they spring from individuals of high ideals.

Guru, the Transcendental Leader:

Ralph Waldo Emerson – American essayist, philosopher, and poet – aptly called the 'Founding Father of Transcendentalist

Movement', defines transcendental leadership as *"an original relation to the Universe."* William Wordsworth goes one step ahead and observes that *"it is a heart that watches and receives."*

Guru was a 'Transcendental Leader'. A Transcendental Leader is concerned for his followers and motivates them and keeps them always empowered. He would be reflective, value oriented, global in perspective, and a facilitator of dialogue. Transcendent leadership provides a revolutionary frame of viewing human interaction in organisational settings. As the society is shifting from old to new paradigms, we are gradually progressing towards transcendental leadership.

A transcendental leader focuses on the transaction and benefits brought upon for the benefits of his subordinates. Such a leader cares more about others than himself. He would motivate and transform the individuals and social systems positively and transform the subordinates into leaders and leadership qualities. The Transcendental Leader is – quite away from both the transactional and transformational types of leaders – concerned for his/her followers always.

Guru evolved a unitive vision of the whole of the mind and its universe, contemplating intensely for year upon year, and then, and for the benefit of others, he divided his unitive awareness into major categories using a scientific methodology. "This type of word production, where wisdom emerges from a holistic appreciation that transcends linear thinking is called **Darsana**. It is a philosophically presented mystic vision" (Guru Nitya Chaitanya Yati). It is an epiphany of ideas.

Guru, the Designer of the 20th Century:

Sree Narayana Guru is the Manager of the 20th Century and his literary creations and preaching are "High-end Management Solutions". Guru re-defined the existing social hierarchy, and worked for abolishing the anti-social and sectarian ideals. His very being, preachings, and every thought were concentrating on a 'Flat System' where the social pyramid created by Brahminical hegemony lost its concept and growth.

The Pyramidal Caste System practised by Aryans:

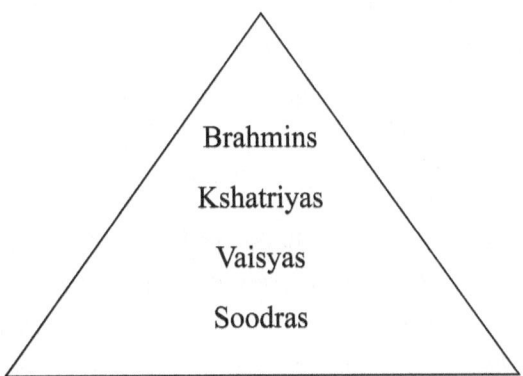

The social stratification on the basis of caste system in Hindu Religion created a hierarchy in the society. This "Hierarchy is dysfunctional and hence it must go", was the attitude of Guru. Instead, the Guru pronounced a novel system of society: "One Caste, One Religion, and One God for Mankind". It is a high-end Social Pyramid.

The Social Pyramid Proposed by Guru:

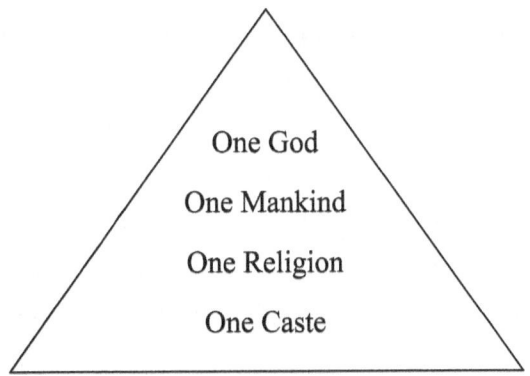

The 'Guru-Factor' may integrate the great figures and join regions apart in time and space, ancient or modern, East or West.

Guru, the Best HR Manager:

Guru shared the maxim: "*Manushyanam Manishyathvam…*" It elaborates: "Be a Human and a Humane…" The Gurujian phrase radiates the celestial light that one man becomes a human being, in the high end origin of 'Homo Sapien' gene, only when he attains humanity – the quality that encompasses virtues like compassion, empathy, love, and nobility…" As one who endeavoured to place the human being at the centre of everything, Guru believed that 'Self –improvement' (development of *Atman*) by individuals was the only hope for society and the world. Another mould-breaking cast of Guru, "*Mathamethayalum Manushyan Nannayal Mathi*" (whatever be the Religion or Caste, let man develop), is the core and pith of 'HR *Manthra*' which ebbs and flows in the perennial ocean of cosmic and cosmopolitan brotherhood, to keep the rhythm of life in the Globe. The human languages run short to narrate the innate, intrinsic, implied meanings of Gurujian phrases, so that, they remain the known unknowns just yet. Let 'emojis' appear to 'drive-them-home' at least to the new generation.

Guru could place a large chunk of people from the bottom of the pyramid to the main stream of economic development. Romain Rolland had put up the statistical calculus that *"the Guru Sree Narayana, whose beneficent spiritual activity has been exercising its influence in the State of Travancore…on nearly two millions of his followers…He was, one might say, a 'Jnani of action'…who had a keen living sense of the people and of social necessities. He has contributed greatly to the elevation of the oppressed classes in south India and his work has been associated, at certain times, with that of Gandhi"* (September 07,2013. *Gurudevan.net*).

Bringing the largest faction of Hindus, say Ezhavas, and the OBC-OEC-SC-ST groups in Kerala – which altogether comes around 57% or more of the Population – spread scattered in the bottom and at the lower middle of the population pyramid of the State of Kerala then, to the main stream of 'education-health-agriculture-industry-and service sectors', was the much acclaimed Human Capital Formation exercise in the peninsular India, under the guardianship of Guru.

Sree Narayana Guru, in the pronouncement of Romain Rolland, was a *'Jnani of Karma (scholar of action),'* who demonstrated how faith can be used to engineer social change. Guru can be rightly qualified as **"The Renaissance Prophet"**, (as coined by B. Ashok. IAS, *hindustantimes.com*, March 13, 2013.)

The website reads: "The Guru's words, deeds, and philosophy acted so forcefully in Indian society that it ushered in a profound cultural renaissance in the increasingly decadent practice of Hindu worship, pock market with animal sacrifices, absurdly severe un-touchability and resultant societal under-achievement. The Guru consecrated 60 odd temples and was farsighted enough to develop Sanskrit, Malayalam, and English schools in almost all of them. They ushered in the renaissance which made Kerala a front runner in literacy and education, resulting in longer life spans and better public health in the country."

Social historians describe the Guru as the vanguard of Kerala society's renaissance; leftists say Guru as the torch-bearer of rationalism; and the agnostics consider him to be the touchstone of rational scepticism. Many backward castes like Ezhavas consider him and his life to be a source of intense and sometimes chauvinistic pride, while for serious students of modern philosophy he is a great practitioner of refined *advaita*.

Guru's ashrams in Shivagiri, Alwaye, and Aruvippuram were thronged by thousands who sought his blessings and words of consolation.

The Guru popularised the ideal where mankind thrives in brotherhood sans the divisions of caste and religion. His unitary absolutism would lead him to declare *"One Caste, One Religion, and One God for Mankind."*

As an epitome of kindliness, he generated such faith that Kerala accepted his gentle counsel as commandments of an absolutist. Emancipator and spiritualist, advaitin and social activist, poet and yogi, the Guru's achievement is both un-paralleled and un-equalled.

It was Sree Narayana Guru's efforts, along with other social reformers and Mahatma Gandhi, which stemmed mass conversions in the late 1890s and led to the opening up of public places, including temples, to all Hindus, irrespective of their caste, in Kerala.

The Guru's literary creations – numbering around 60 + 1* renditions – in chaste Sanskrit, erudite Tamil, and lucid Malayalam are projecting testimony to his scholarly height and reach as an exponent of post-Sankara *Advoita* or **"Absolute Idealism"** as it is understood by western philosophers. Guru – a pure non-dualist – had held an equi-distant philosophy from all religions and faiths.

The significance of the Guru is in taking the *vedic* ideal and changing society with it irreversibly and non-violently. Guru's *Vedantic* Ideals in *Darśana Mālā* is a "Blue Sky Strategy" for Indian social changes and it can be used for a new social order across the world, as well. Like the 'blue sky' it is so vast and deep and powerful and summarizes the distinct characteristics so as to compete the passé 'Red Ocean Philosophy' of feudalism, un-touchability and other social taboos. (indebted to *BLUE OCEAN STRATEGY* written by W.Chan Kim and Renee Mauborgne, Harvard Business Review Press, 2004, United States). As Mao observed once, while referring to the French Revolution, "*the impact of that first step is still fuelling the winds of change in the nation*", the Guru's words and deeds in the State are still a clarion call for change in the Country. (B. Ashok IAS, "*The Guru of social reforms*, 13 March 2013, gurudevan.net)

* The 61st literary creation is "*Subrahmania Sthuthy.*" A dispute exists regarding its authorship.(Narayana Guru, Sampoorna Krithikai, Narayana Gurukulam, Sreenivasapuram P.O, Varkala, Karala).

Educating for Growth:

Guru had had all the attributes of a responsible entrepreneur. He recognised human capital as crucial wealth for economic growth and social progress. A healthy, literate and skilled populace is vital for manufacturing, services, agriculture, and industry. The World Bank Report 2018 shows that India ranks 115th in the Human Capital Index (HCI) – below every South Asian country except Afghanistan and Pakistan. Education is the core factor behind human capital formation. Guru had recognised it years ago. "*A scholar sees; a seer sees through.*"

"Give not the fish, but the net" to the poor strata was Guru's take on poverty alleviation. Education is the basic and rudimentary '*sine-qua-non*' for individual development. Not *bhakti,* but *yukti* must be the forerunner. Educate the down-trodden first. So, Guru opened many schools; then the temples; then again the schools. The prioritisation of the Guru to fight against the social evils amassed momentum. "*Enlighten Through Education*" – the rocky slogan of the Guru – reverberated on and out-passed the Western Ghats and the Aravalli, and echoed down the Himalayas.

Guru and Corporate Social Responsibility:

Guru's signature quote, *"Avanavan – atma –Sughathin – aa – charikkunnava – Apārannu – sughathinayi – varenam"* is the exact replica of his social consciousness and it conveys the invaluable concept of Social Responsibility. The 'Three Ps theory of modern management – Profits Making, Planet (Environment) Keeping, and Public (Social) Development has been beautifully incorporated in his **"Pancha Sudhi,"**, **"Pancha Dharma,"** and **"Pancha Maha Yajna"** Concepts. These concepts focus on self-regulations that aim to contribute to societal goals of philanthropic, activist, or charitable nature. They engage in or support volunteering or ethically oriented practices for general welfare.

Distributed Leadership:

Well before it was even thought of in the new millennium business management, Guru proposed the philosophy of Distributed Leadership. It is concerned with the practice of leadership rather than specific leadership roles and responsibilities. It equates with shared, collective, and extended leadership practice that builds the capacity for change and improvement. The authority does not being held by one person, but is instead distributed among multiple individuals, or a body of leadership, which has many individuals who have the tools and skills to the success of the organisation. The Management of *"Sree Narayana Dharma Paripalana Yogam (SNDP Yogam)* is the arch example of the "Management By Distributed Leadership." When Guru was at the helm of SNDP Yogam, he practiced the authority and power to love and to make a bond among the members. It can be qualified as *"Guru Effect in Management."*

The Guru's Distributed Leadership idea can be detected in the recent Book **"New Power": How it's changing the 21st century – and why you need to know"**, by Henry Timms and Jeremy Heimans (19 April 2018, Pan Macmillan).

"Power is the ability to produce intended effects," coined Bertrand Russel. The human history clearly tells us the rules of power. Power was something to be seized, and then jealously guarded and kept it. Under the old power, we lived in a world of rulers and subjects. Now we all sense that something has changed. Why outsiders are winning, institutions are failing, and how the rest of us can keep up in the age of 'Mass Participation.'

Old power is held by few, kept and closed, inaccessible and leader-driven. It downloads and captures. New power, whereas, is open, participatory, and peer-driven. It uploads, distributes, disseminates, and channelize to society. Old power models demand us to comply with, whereas the new power models ask us to share and create. The power to hold is old; and the power to share is that of new. *"The power is of two kinds. One is obtained by the fear of punishment and the other by acts of love. Power based on love is a thousand times more effective and permanent than the one derived from fear of punishment."* (MK Gandhi, Sacred Space, The Times Of India, Saturday, February 8, 2020} The "Mass Participation and Care and Share" were the irrefutable dictums of Guru.

Purpose-over-Personalities Mantra: Guru used the 'purpose-*over-personalities*' mantra to lead the *"Navodhana Movement"* in South India and taught straight forward business ethics to the seat-of-the-pants leaders and rulers. Business schools may pursue students for a case study on Guru's leadership style. Implementing it the multi-nationals can better manage their star-studded teams and factions; avoid management feuds that often rock the corporate world.

Development Religion:

Guru's ground-breaking, experiment-based, extensive empirical research and the innovative field experiment led him to pronounce "Development Religion." The Guru's religion is Development Religion. Guru has shown how the problem of religious tyranny can be tackled by breaking it down into a number of smaller – but more precise – issues at caste and sub-caste levels. This approach in the field level led into the mass theory of "Development Religion." Guru proclaimed: *"whatever be the Religion of man, let him develop."* For the development of man, Guru advised to forgo the religion and accept education; do agriculture and industry; learn foreign languages; imbibe technology; and inculcate cleanliness. "The micro-level individual development would deliver a steady flow in the macro-level societal renaissance in the country", was the focus of Guru.

There had long been an awareness of the huge differences in average productivity between the affluent upper castes and the deprived and the 'les miserables' of the down castes. There had always been a confrontation between the "Control Group" of upper-castes and the "Intervention Group" of the down castes. The feud would render un-touchability, poverty, social tyranny, and the resultant under-development of the economy as a whole. Guru's life and His total being were for an extensive-empirical-filed-research against the social menace of economic under-development of the nation. In a crucial analysis, one may ask, "Is it the essence of the innovative ground-breaking, experiment-based research in to '**how to reduce global poverty?**' for which the Indian-American economist Abhijit Banerjee won the 2019 Nobel Prize in Economic Sciences, with his colleague and French-American wife Esther Duflo, of MIT, along with fellow-American economist Michael Kremer of the Harvard?"

Why "The Royal Swedish Academy of Sciences" failed/ fails to pave a berth at its Gallery of Laureates for the Guru and Gandhiji? Perhaps they might be thinking that the duo is much ahead of such decorations. Both – the Apostle of non-violence and the Monarch of Renaissance – were and had been much ahead of any humanly, nay worldly, decorations!! And Thomas Gray's Elegy echoes...

"Full many a gem of purest ray serene,
The dark unfathomed caves of ocean bear;
Full many a flower is born to blush unseen,
And waste its sweetness on the desert air."

Health, education, *Pancha Shuddhi*, (five cleanliness) *Pancha Dharma* (five right behaviours), and *Pancha Maha Yajna* (five daily worships) of Guru, like Gandhi"'s "charka-thread-Khadi, and salt", were very basic and rudimentary which would have concrete effects on common man, positively and effectively. Much were there in common between Gandhi and Guru. Had the Guru been born anywhere in the Hindi-belt of India, the duo would have been 'First Class First' and could have done still better.

Remedial Economics:

Religion must ring out; Development must ring in. Temple entry would give a short term benefit, but education would render perennial results. "Education, adoption of new technology, learning of foreign languages, agriculture-industry-service orientation, ardent co-operation (Yogam), and the united action" would be the sources for long term and perspective plans for life-long growth and prosperity – advised Guru. "Big ideas do matter. They produce a coherent economic vision which can guide us. Keep social taboos and animal sacrifices at bay.

Reading Scriptures and Vedas would enlighten the ignoramus. Work as a 'Movement.' Pragmatic scepticism and willingness to question shall be the foundation of all your movements. Free of fear and doubts, science in the place of nescience, practice of truth and ahimsa," were the glittering and glaring pieces of Guru's teachings.

The *Sree Narayana Dharma Paripalana (SNDP) Yogam*, with the guidance and blessings of Sree Narayana Guru, *was* founded on 15 May 1903, and registered as a Public Limited Company under the Indian Companies Act, 1882. Guru was its first and the life-long President. Dr. Palpu was its vice-president; 'Mahakavi' Kumaran Asan its secretary. The history of SNDP Yogam is the rise of the socially backward, depressed classes in Kerala. It is the social development of Ezhavas from mere owner of '*thalappu and ladder*' (according to the Royal Order, 824, of Maharaja of Travancore) to the present state. The history of SNDP *Yogam* is the shining story of the vertical-horizontal change of an almost food-gathering society into a cosmopolitan world order.

"The Yogam is the first Organisation which envisaged Kerala as a whole. It was considered to be the largest and the most prominent Public Organisation in the South Region of the Nation." (gurudevan.net).

A plethora of Organisations sprout up in Kerala, under the blessings of the Guru. They were aimed at the total emancipation of the deprived and the down-trodden strata in the erstwhile Princely States of Malabar, Kochi, and Travancore. The 10 major movements, under the aegis of Sree Narayana Guru and/ in his name, which were instrumental for the total Renaissance in Kerala, could be put up chronologically as:

Aruvippuram Temple Society (1888)
Aruvippuram Kshetra Yogam (1888)
Ezhava Sabha (1896)
Ezhava Memorial to the Maharaja of Travancore (3 Sept 1896)
Sree Narayana Dharma Paripalana Yogam (1903)
The Sivagiri Mutt (1904)
The Brahma Vidyalaya (1924)
The Sree Narayana Dharma Sangham Trust (1926, inc. in 1928)
The Sree Narayana Trusts (January 31 1952)
Sree Narayana Sevika Samaj (1965)

These institutional stalwarts in the Nation have been manoeuvring their roles in Human Capital Formation of high order. They are the material proofs of the cosmopolitan visions of Guru Sree Narayana, the 20th century link of the Maharishis' clan of Bharat.

"Seven thousand years of India's pre-history and twenty centuries of recorded history make their claim on Narayana Guru as the renascent re-creator of India's past and present culture. As an erudite scholar of the ancient Pali and Sanskrit languages and a reformer of the regional languages of Tamil and Malayalam, the Guru gave new insight into the world wisdom of India's Vedic lore and Upanishedic Profundity. His affiliation to the spiritual insight of Vedanta (India's Brahminic lore) and Siddhanta (Dravidian ethnic wisdom lore) was of a dedicated son of India's native soil."

"He fought with his inspired pen of poetic lyric to liberate his downtrodden contemporaries who had been reduced to the status of domestic slaves and illiterates for more than four millennia. His path of liberation was of soul-freeing education and service to fellow humans as a model for shouldering responsibilities as compassionate citizens of a new world culture and ethos". (www.narayanagurukula.org)

Gandhi – Guru Duo:

Perhaps, the great unfortunate absence or missing in Indian history might be the absence of 'Guru-Gandhi Duo' and their united attempts for the total emancipation of the nation from the clutches of the religious divide and the consequential outcomes. *'The whole could have been greater than the sum of its parts.'*

There were many commonalities between them. When Gandhiji advocated for *'non-violence and peace'*, Guru propounded *'Pancha Shuddhi'*; when Gandhi called for *'ahimsa'*, Guru propagated *'Pancha Dharma'; and w*hen Gandhiji stood for *'satyahraha'*, Guru perpetuated *'Pancha Yjna.'*

[*Panch Shuddhi*: i.e., keeping cleanliness with regard to the five items in day-to-day life – body, words, mind, senses, and home].

[*Pancha Dharma*: i.e., keeping five principles in everyday life – ahimsa, sathyam (truth), astheyam (non-stealing) avyabhicharam (non-lust), and maddya varjanam (prohibition)].

[*Pancha Maha Yajna*: i.e., performance of five Duties in day-to-day being – *Brahma Yajnam* (learning spiritual texts), *Pitru Yajnam* (respect parents, teachers, and elders), *Daiva Yajnam* (offer prayers to God), *Bhoota Yajnam* (love environment and care its flora and fauna), *Manushya Yajnam* (love fellow country-men)].

Questioned Vedic Belief:

Sree Narayana Guru questioned the Vedic belief system of India. The system had become increasingly ritualistic, susceptible to mis-interpretations, which supported certain power structures in India. Martin Luther King's 'Protestantism' essentially led a crusade against the existing belief system of the Church. Lincoln's anti-slavery movement questioned the slavery system in the US. Mahatma Gandhi's Ahimsa Movement fought against the 'Colonial power' of Britain and won freedom for India. Nelson Mandela's Anti-Apartheid movement questioned the colour apartheid in South Africa. All these are the caste/religious based disruptive movements across the world.

Buddha 'knew' that 'desire' was the cause of sorrow, and the sorrow could be destroyed by 'overpowering desires.' Lincoln 'knew' that the greatest social evil was slavery and he led the 'Abolition and Anti-slavery Movement' against it and won over the evil. Martin Luther King 'knew' that the Church had become corrupt and he was daring enough to nail his 'Ninety Five Theses' on to the door of the chapel in Wittenberg, Germany, which changed the Christian World. Mahatma Gandhi 'knew' that fighting against Colonial power was a futile exercise and he developed the 'Spiritual Might' of Indians manifested in 'Satyagraha' and won Independence. Nelson Mandela 'knew' that the Apartheid (separateness of Africans) was the destructive evil and his 'Anti-apartheid Movement' resorted to 'Internal Resistance and Passive Resistance' to apartheid and fought against the forcible relocation of Africans of colour and won freedom for the Blacks. Guru 'knew' that the 'Casteism and Untouchability' stand tall pausing a stumbling block in social development of the 'lower castes' in India, and he organised the 'Les Miserables' against it and won over the evil.

"One caste, One Religion, and One God for Mankind", was a Disruptive Slogan against Casteism in India. It simply challenged the existing power structure based on brahminical tyranny. "Be Educated; Be Liberals", Guru resumed. The Guru's wise-sayings reverberate through the ages – past, present, and yet to come.

A Green Answer to a Blue Question:

The Guru consecrated 'Siva Idol' at Aruvippuram. Installation of idols by non-Brahmins was considered blasphemy, those days. It was an act of challenging the age-old Brahminic hegemony, so that, the Brahmin priests questioned the Guru's right to do so. The calm and cool Guru bestowed that it was 'Ezhava Siva' that he consecrated.' *'An action is important but the reaction is all the more important',* Guru proved. The Brahmin priests were gagged, reminding that 'the slow and steady experiences energy flow.' Those born to emancipate just cut through the problems that come in their way. The Guru cut the Gordian knot using his graceful wisdom.

Sensing the prevailing caste-system, Swami Vivek Ananda qualified Kerala the 'Lunatic Asylum', but the epoch making activities of Guru transformed it in to a modern scientific region, nowadays heard as "God's Own Country", world over.

Relationship Management:

The Guru roused the stunner in the followers. He advised them to move from ugliness to beauty, monstrosity to saintliness, parochialism to pragmatism, and from injustice to justice. "Symbiosis, synergy, and sustainability" is the pith and core of his teachings. It is, closely watching, the most affluent elements in modern 'Relationship Management.' It is the 'Power of Bonding." He advised not to inflict or vex even an ant; rear love, instead." The ancient Greeks gave this love a name. They called it 'agape' (ah-gah-pay) to distinguish it from romantic love, familial love, or love of one's country. *Agape* is the love that celebrates the indivisible oneness of all humanity, regardless of any distinction of religion, race, gender, or nationality. It is the Godly love towards all beings and covers both flora and fauna. It is the closest that we can get to an intimation of that which is divine. Or, to put it as vector Hugo said, *"To love another is to see the face of God."*

Oh! Great Lord Divine...
In the deep ocean of your Glory
Let us all become immersed;
There to dwell, dwell forever
In Felicity Supreme!!

(Part B)

Tagorian Take on Sree Narayana Guru

Rabindranath Tagore visited Guru in his Ashram at Sivagiri on 22nd November 1922 and paid homage: *"I have been touring different parts of the world. During these travels, I have had the fortune to come into contact with several saints and maharishis. But I have frankly to admit that I have never seen one who is spiritually greater than Swamy Narayana Guru of Malayalam – nay, a person who is on par with him in spiritual attainment"*.

"I am sure, I shall never forget that radiant face illuminated by the self effulgent light of divine glory and those majestic eyes fixing their gaze on far remote point in the distant horizon." (*Gurudevan.net*)

Mahatma Gandhi's Ode to Sree Narayana Guru

Mahatma Gandhi called at Sivagiri Mutt and called on Guru on 12 March 1925. On his return Gandhiji remarked: *"I feel it as the greatest privilege in my life to have visited the beautiful State of Travancore and to have a darshan of Venerable sage His Holiness Sree Narayana Guru. I had the fortune to stay one day in his holy Asramam...His Holiness told me yesterday that we might not see the end of this agony (caste–discrimination) during our life time, in this generation, and that I should have to wait for another incarnation of mine before I had the pleasure of seeing the end of this agony. I respectfully differed from him. I hope to see the end in this very age during my life time, but I do not hope to do so without your assistance. Assist me to the full measure of your ability to show you that this wrong becomes a thing of the past. Do your duty manfully and I undertake to show to you that this fifth class from Hinduism entirely scraped... I tender my thanks publicly to His Holiness for the extreme kindness that he has shown to me and the hospitality that he has extended to me. I thank you once more for the address that you have presented to me and for the patience with which you have listened to me, but the best reward that I ask you to give me, I expect, is the translation of what you have listened to in action."* (*Gurudevan.net*)

Although Gandhiji was against un-touchability, he believed in the *Varnashrama* system. Citing the example of the difference in the sizes of the leaves of the same tree, Gandhiji stated that different *varnas* (classes of people) did exist naturally. Gurudevan replied with the same example that though the sizes of the leaves may be different, they all taste the same. Just like the same sap runs through leaves of different shapes, the people said to be belonging to different castes are the manifestations of the same reality. This simple illustration changed Ganghiji's mind-set about the *varna* system.

Rollandian Rhyme on Guru

The French Scholar (writer, philosopher, dramatist, novelist, essayist, art historian and mystic, who won the Nobel Prize for literature in 1915) had registered his will on Sree Narayana Guru thus: "Glasenapp does not say anything regarding the new religious manifestations in South India which are not negligible: such for example is *the great Guru, Sree Narayana, whose beneficent spiritual activity has been exercising its influence during the past forty years in the State of Travancore on nearly two millions of his followers. His teaching, permeated with the philosophy of Sankara, shows evidence of a striking difference of temperament compared with the mysticism of Bengal, of which the effusions of love (bhakti) inspire in him a certain mistrust. He was, one might say, a Jnani of action, a grand religious intellectual, who had a keen living sense of the people and of social necessities. He has contributed greatly to the elevation of the oppressed classes in south India, and his work has been associated at certain times with that of Gandhi." (September 07, 2013. Gurudevan.net)*

Theosophical Society about Guru (September 1928)

"During recent centuries no one in India has enjoyed so much reverence as Sree Narayana Gurudev commanded, reverence so glorious, so enduring, so comprehensive, so universal and so pure. Like the sun, by mere presence, he spread his light and love…His life of renunciation has shown to numerous people the secret of the path of the dedicated service or karmayoga. Rishi Narayana who has awakened Kerala is Pathanjali in Yoga, Shankara in wisdom, Manu in the art of governance, Buddha in renunciation, Muhammad in strength of spirituality, and Christ in humility, after 72 years spent in the dharma of human life has gone to whence he came…For future generations he will be one of the divine personalities among the incarnations of God and the superhuman being of India's 'Religious Lore.' (https//www.facebook.com/gurudevan.in) (*GURUDEVAN.NET*, September 7, 2013).

Acharya Vinoba Bhave on Guru

Acharya Vinoba Bhave visited Guru in 1926. *"Sree Narayana Guru is considered as one of the five or ten avatars that have appeared in India during the last hundred years. I had an opportunity to meet him when I had been to Kerala for Vaikkom Satyagraha. In those days he was residing at Varkala. There I had talked to him for an hour or two. My humble respect to the memory of this great sage."* (*GURUDEVAN.NET*, September 7, 2013).

Deena Bandhu Charles Freer Andrews' Trait on Guru

"Once C F Andrews, priest of the Church of England, along with Rabindranath Tagore, visited Sree Narayana Guru, at his Ashram at Sivagiri. He observed:

"I had a vision of God in human form, Sree Narayana Guru, who was renowned in the southern-most part of India, was that 'Supreme Being." (*Gurudevan.net*)

Then he wrote to Romain Rolland: *"that I have seen our Christ walking on the shore of Arabian Sea in the attire of a hindu sanyasin."* (*https//en.m.wikipedia.org*)

THE END.

Bibliography

Reference of Books and Authors

Darśanamala (Malayalam)

- Sree Narayana Guru, Full Tex.

Daiva Dasakam (Malayalam)

- The Universal Prayer, Sree Narayana Guru, Full Text.

Atmopadesa Satakam (Malayalam)

- Sree Narayana Guru, Mounam Books, Kottayam, (2002): Full Text.

Bhagavad Gita Vyasa: 3,4,5,7,18, 82–84, 99–102, 120, 157–159, 171–172, 206–208, 271–274, 317–19, 369–70, 401–402, 425, 440–443.

The Bhagavad Gita, Nataraja Guru, R&K Publishing House, Delhi, p. 29, 30, 92, 124, 147, 166, 172, 180, 191, 234–236, 300, 301, 409, 415, 566–569, 590,591, 705.

The Bible, Gospel according to St. John: 1: 1–5

The Bible, Corinthians 5:6

The Bible, Matthew 17:20

The Bible, King James Version, Matthew 7:1.

The Bible, The Gospel According to John, 11. 25–26

The Hebrew Bible, Genesis 12:7

The Bible, Psalm 44:21

The Holy Qur 'an, A. Yusuf Ali (Trans.), American Trust Publication, p14.

Upanishads:

Chandogya 99, 363, 451, 452., and 6.8.7(the dialogue between Uddalaka and his son Swetaketu), Isavasya 205, 207.

Mandukya 59, 258,259.

Taittiriya 146, 152.

Nataraja Guru, An Integrated Science of the Absolute, D.K Print world (p) Ltd, New Delhi, ISBN13: 9788124601860, vii, xii, 6, 7, 10, 11, 14, 15.

Guru Nitys Chaitanya Yati, (1987), *The Psychology of Darśana Mālā,* Gurukula Publishing House, Fernhill-Varkala-Bainbridge, Full Text.

Nataraja Guru, *An anthology of the poems of Narayana Guru,* Trans. Nataraja Guru, vii, p26–27.

Kuttikalute Narayana Guru, (Malayalam)

 – Swami Muni Narayana Prasad, (1999), Narayana Gurukulam publication, Varkala, Kerala, Full Text.

Sree Narayana Gurudevan, (Malayalam)

 – N. Ramankutty, (1998), Kavithraya Publications, Peringottukara, Thrissur, p35–44, 92, 137–150.

YOGESWARANAYA SREE NARAYANA GURU,(Malayalam)

- A R Sreenivasan, (1997), Kurukshethra Prakasan Pvt Ltd, p36–37, 68–70.

GURUDEVA CHARITHRA KADHAKALILE KANAPPURANGAL (Essays), (Malayalam)

- Swami Sachidanada,(2004), Second Edition, Divine Printers, Chalakkudy, Kerala, p9–12, 34–35, 93.

GURUDEVANTE SATHYADARŚANAM, (Malayalam)

- Swami Saswathik ĀNANDA, (1992), Current Books, p31–34, 137–140.

Narayana Guru SAMPOORNA KRITHIKAL(Complete works of Narayaan Guru), (Malayalam)

- *First Narayana Gurukulam Edition, (2004),* Chaitanya Publishers, Ulloor, Thiruvanathapuram, p8–10, 149–168.

General Readings:

Sakichi Toyoda, (1930), *Five Whys Analysis.*

Smith,Bill., (1980), *Six Sigma Techniques.*

Masaaki Imai, (1986*), Kizen: The Key to Japan's Competitive Success.*

Humphrey, Albert S., (1960s), *SWOT Analysis.*

Drucker, Peter F., (1986), *Management Theories.*

W. Chan Kim and Renee Mauborgue, (2004), **Blue Ocean Strategy:** *How to Create Uncontested Market Space and Make the Competition Irrelevent.*

Whitman, Walt., (1855), *Song of Myself,* Dover Publication, America.

Hemingway, Earnest.,(1932), *Death in the Afternoon.*

Barrie, James Matthew., (1953), *Peter Pan.*

Rostow, Walt Whitman., (1960), *The Stages of Economic Growth: A Non-Communist Manifesto,* Cmbridge University Press.

Maslow, Abraham., (1943*), A Theory of Human Motivation,* Essay.

BCG Matrix, The Boston Consulting Group.

Blake, Robert Rogers., and Mouton, Jane Srygley., America, (1964), *The Managerial Grid Model (Leadership Matrix).*

General Magazine:

Maurer, Stephen B., (March 2, 1980), *The King Chicken Theorems,* Mathematics Magazine, Mathematical Association of America.

Web Sites:

Chanakya Sutra (the second *Sutra*), *echanakya.blogspot.com*

Small Business Administration (SBA), USA, *www.sba.gov.*

https://www.speakingtrees, *Times of India.*

Baruch Spinoza, *en.m.wikipedia.org*

Gurudevan.net

https//www.facebook.com/gurudevan.in

https//en.m.wikipedia.org

September7, 2013, GURUDEVAN.NET.

The Commentator

VISWANATHAN. C.N. was born in 1957, in Kottayam Dist., Kerala, India. After his Post Graduation (M.Com) from the University of Kerala, he joined as Lecturer in the 'Post Graduate Department of Commerce and Management Studies' at **Sree Narayana College, Nattika**, Kerala, in 1983.

Subsequently, he was Commissioned into National Cadet Corps (Army Wing), India, in 1986.

M.A. Eco., PGDHRM, MBA, and Ph.D are his afterwards acquisitions.

Putting 32 years of yeoman service in Indian Higher Educational-cum-Regimental realms, he retired in March, 2014.

Assumed the post of Director – Ahalia School of Management – under Ahalia International Foundation, in June, 2014.

Adjunct Faculty of Kerala Police Academy (KEPA), Thrissur, Kerala, since its inception in 1999.

Chairman of Academic Council at Nattika Educational Society (NES), a leading Charitable-cum-Higher Educational Institution in Kerala.

Presently he is the Principal of the largest Self Financing College – CET College of Management, Science, and Technology – Airapuram, Ernakulam Dist., Kerala.

The present work is his maiden voyage.

The Brief of the Present Work

NOT TO ARGUE AND WIN BUT TO KNOW AND TO BE KNOWN – A Blue Sky Strategy – is a book on Management and Philosophy.

Brahmarshi Sree Narayana Guru (28 August 1855 – 20 September 1928) convened and graced 'The International Religious Congress' at Aluva, in Kerala, in February 1924. **His All – Holiness Guru** pronounced the Canon of Love as a slogan of the Congress: **"WE MEET HERE NOT TO ARGUE AND WIN BUT TO KNOW AND TO BE KNOWN."** The slogan reverberated across the Globe crossing the Himalayas and the Indian Ocean.

The author, honestly and most indebtedly, borrowed the *Mahamantra* to be decorated at the present work as its pendant.

The Great *Rishi* has 61 literary-mystic-philosophical creations in His credit of which ***Darśana Mālā*** is the ***Magnum Opus***. It contains Ten ***Darśanas*** of the 'profoundest-mystical-intrinsic-intricacies' so as to qualify it as ***Bhagavad Gita 2.0.***

The author of the present work has accomplished his endeavour to 'Transform' the energy contained in the Ten *Darśanas* to analogise and to equate them to '*Ten Management Sutras.*'

And, honourably hope that ***The Guru Darśanas*** are the high-end Epiphany of Management Thoughts; those who follow them shall surf in the up-above Blue Sky of success. Hence it is *A Blue Sky Strategy.*

Shall we submit it at the lotus feet of the *Jagat Guru.*

AUM TAT SAT

Index

General Index